Financial Management

Dr.N. Prakash

Dr.M. Yasotha

Dr.M. Vidhya

Published by

BONFRING®
Intellectual Integrity

Financial Management

9 789387 862289 >

ISBN 978-93-87862-28-9

Authors

Dr.N. Prakash

Dr.M. Yasotha

Dr.M. Vidhya

Bonfring

309, 2nd Floor,

5th Street Extension, Gandhipuram, Coimbatore-641 012.

Tamilnadu, India.

E-mail: info@bonfring.org

Website: www.bonfring.org

Phone: 0422 4213231

Authors Profile

Dr.N. Prakash, serves as Associate professor in KV institute of Management and Information Studies, Coimbatore. He was conferred with Ph.D in Management by Bharathiar University His corporate stint comprised services at Religare, Karvy, Bajaj capital, and JRG. He is specialized in Financial Service sector and having a good experience in those field for nearly 4 years and he is associated with teaching for More than 6 Years. His area of interest is, Mutual funds, Financial statement analysis and Financial planning.

To add on with the research credentials he published in various International Journals like Asian Journal of Research in Social Sciences and Humanities, Scholars World, IJAMBU, SAJOSPS, Journal of Management Science. Attended various FDP programs such as SPSS, AMOS and in IIM-K Financial Statement Analysis. He is a trainer for NISM courses. His research is focused on financial services especially in Mutual funds. He conducted an FDP on Financial Statement Analysis.

Dr.M. Yasotha working as an Associate Professor at KV Institute of Management and Information Studies, Coimbatore, who has an academic experience of over 12 years. Apart from that she also served in National Service Scheme around 10 years. Her areas of interest include Share trading and Micro finance. To her credit, she published quality papers in various peer reviewed journals. She has often been known to spend hours at financial meetings helping students to understand her unique financial methodologies in the area of mutual funds, share trading and financial analysis. She has actively organized seminars and Guest lectures. She has attended more number of FDPs, MDPs and International Conferences. Her long term vision is to become soft skill trainer through which to accelerate the young minds.

Dr.M. Vidhya is a Professor and Principal of KV Institute of Management and Information Studies, with an experience of 18 Years in academic and administration. She completed her Ph.D. at Bharathiar University. Her research interest lies in the area of Finance and Marketing. she has got an active collaboration with researchers worldwide. She has presented papers at conferences both at home and abroad, published articles and papers in various reputed journals and contributed to the book "Marketing Management". Leadership, teamwork, Interview skills and other financial topics are prominent among her delivery. She has taught number of courses on HR, Finance, Marketing over the years. Over the last ten years, she has been prominent administrator of KV Institute of Management as principal and leading the institute. She has served roughly fifty conferences and workshop, in program committees and served as the program chair for various events. Importantly, she has designed the application-oriented curriculum in HR, Marketing and Finance for the welfare of the students to gain the industrial exposure. Despite administration activities, she is continuing her research and been guiding the research scholars.

Syllabus

BA5203 **FINANCIAL MANAGEMENT** **LTPC**

4004

Objectives

Facilitate student to

- Understand the operational nuances of a Finance Manager
- Comprehend the technique of making decisions related to finance function

Chapter 1: Foundations of Finance 9

Introduction to finance - Financial Management – Nature, scope and functions of Finance, organization of financial functions, objectives of Financial management, Major financial decisions – Time value of money – features and valuation of shares and bonds – Concept of risk and return – single asset and of a portfolio.

Chapter 2: Investment Decisions 9

Capital Budgeting: Principles and techniques - Nature of capital budgeting- Identifying relevant cash flows - Evaluation Techniques: Payback, Accounting rate of return, Net Present Value, Internal Rate of Return, Profitability Index - Comparison of DCF techniques Concept and measurement of cost of capital - Specific cost and overall cost of capital.

Chapter 3: Financing and Dividend Decision 9

Leverages - Operating and Financial leverage – measurement of leverages – degree of Operating & Financial leverage – Combined leverage, EBIT – EPS Analysis- Indifference point.

Capital structure – Theories – Net Income Approach, Net Operating Income Approach, MM Approach – Determinants of Capital structure.

Dividend decision- Issues in dividend decisions, Importance, Relevance & Irrelevance theories – Walter"s – Model, Gordon"s model and MM model. – Factors determining dividend policy – Types of dividend policies – forms of dividend

Chapter 4: Working Capital Management 9

Principles of working capital: Concepts, Needs, Determinants, issues and estimation of working capital - Accounts Receivables Management and factoring - Inventory management - Cash management - Working capital finance: Trade credit, Bank finance and Commercial paper.

Chapter 5: Long Term Sources of Finance 9

Indian capital and stock market, New issues market Long term finance: Shares, debentures and term loans, lease, hire purchase, venture capital financing, Private Equity.

Total: 45 Periods

Chapter	Contents	Page No

CHAPTER 1

FOUNDATIONS OF FINANCE

1.1. Introduction to Finance

Finance is defined as the provision of money at the time when it is required. Every enterprise, whether big, medium, small, needs finance to carry on its operations and to achieve its target. In fact, finance is so indispensable today that it is rightly said to be the blood of an enterprise. Without adequate finance, no enterprise can possibly accomplish its objectives.

Finance is one of the requisites for all human activities like, personal, business or government. Finance refers to the money resources owned or borrowed available to individuals, business or governments for their operations. Basically, finance is monetized form of capital, and capital is the saving for investment. Amount of savings depends on income and consumption. There are certain macro economics equations.

$$Y=C+S; \qquad Y=C+I; \qquad S=I$$

Meaning of Financial Management: Financial management refers to that part of the management activity, which is concerned with the planning, & controlling of firm's financial resources. It deals with finding out various sources for raising funds for the firm. Financial management is practiced by many corporate firms and can be called Corporation finance or Business Finance.

Definition of Finance

George Chirsty and Peter Roden observes that, "finance may be generally defined as the study of money, its nature, creation, behaviour, regulation and problems"

Finance may be defined as, "the provision of at the time when it is required" Finance refers to the management of flows of money through an organization.

Weston and Brigham "Financial management is an area of financial decision making harmonizing individuals motives and enterprise goals"

Functions of Finance

- Business functions
- Focus of all activities
- It is not possible to substitute
- Money is continuous
- Setting up of an enterprise

- Development and expansion of business
- The fund will have to raised from various sources
- The inflows and outflows of the funds should be properly matched.

Nature of Finance

- The finance is in-substitutable and is a focus of all activities. The need for finance is increase in the development of business.
- Money is formally the most rational means of economic activities.
- Money will have to be procured and funds will have to be raised
- The establishment of most organization is the procurement of money contribution.
- Money contributions may vary in many ways.
- There are many ways of procuring funds and decisions on this matter are based on a wide range of economic, legal and organizational consideration.
- It is an effective utilization of funds. Commitments of funds are well justified.
- Finance function is very sensitive to time dimension.

Scope of Finance

- It concentrates primarily on money management
- It concentrates the different auxiliaries which are incidental to it.
- It relates to product pricing, expansion, the acquisition of new concern etc.
- It is closely inter-related with other areas of business operations.
- It should be remembered that both production and distribution.
- It may be extended to the chief activities involving a successful administration of finance.
- It may be divided into financial planning, financing and public ownership.

1.2. Scope of Financial Management

The approach to the scope and functions of financial management is divided, for purposes of exposition, into two broad categories: (a) The traditional approach and (b) The modern Approach.

Traditional Approach

The traditional approach to the scope of financial management refers to its subject matter, in academic literature in the initial stages of its evolution, as a separate branch of academic study. The term 'corporate finance' was used to describe what is now known in the academic world as 'financial management'.

In other words, the scope of the finance function was treated by meet their financing needs. The term 'procurement' was used in a broad sense so as to include the whole gamut of raising funds externally. Thus defined, the field of study dealing with finance was treated as encompassing three interrelated aspects of raising and administering resources from outside: (i) the institutional arrangements in the form of financial institutions which comprise the organization of the capital market; (ii) the financial instruments through which funds are raised from the capital markets and the related aspects of practices and the procedural aspects of capital markets; and (iii) the legal and accounting relationships between a firm and its sources of funds.

The weakness of the traditional approach fall into two broad categories: (i) those relating to the treatment of various topics and the emphasis attached to them and (ii) those relating to the basic conceptual and analytical framework of the definitions and scope of the finance function.

Modern Approach

The modern approach views the term financial management in a broad sense and provides a conceptual and analytical framework for financial decision making. According to it, the finance function covers both acquisitions of funds as well as their allocations. Thus, apart from the issues involved in acquiring external funds, the main concern of financial management is the efficient and wise allocation of funds to various uses. Defined in a broad sense, it is viewed as an integral part of overall management.

The new approach is an analytical way of viewing the financial problems of a firm. In other words, the financial management, according to the new approach, is concerned with the solution of three major problems relating to the financial operations of a firm, corresponding to the three questions of investment, financing and dividend decisions. Thus, financial management, in the modern sense of the firm, can be broken down into three major decisions as functions of finance: (i) The investment decision (ii) The financing decision, and (iii) The dividend policy decision.

Investment Decision: The investment decision relates to the selection of assets in which funds will be invested by a firm. The assets which can be acquired fall into two broad groups: (i) long term assets which yield a return over a period of time in future, (ii) shot term or current assets, defined as those assets which in the normal course of business are convertible into cash without diminution in the value, usually within a year. The first of these involving the first category of assets is popularly known in financial literature as capital budgeting. The aspect of financial decision making with reference to current assets or short term assets is popularly termed as working capital management.

1.3. Organization of Finance Functions

ORGANISATION OF THE FINANCE FUNCTION

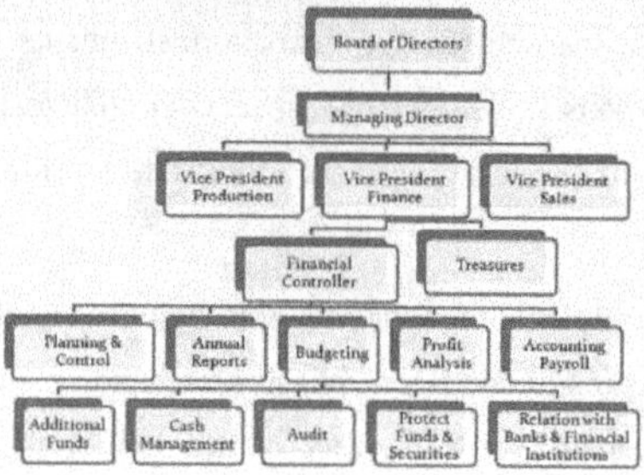

1.4. Definition of Financial Management

According to Guthmann and Dougall: "Business finance can be broadly defined as the activity concerned with the planning, raising controlling and administrating the funds used in the business."

According to Joseph & Massie: "Financial Management is the operational activity of a business that is responsible for obtaining and effectively utilizing the funds necessary for efficient operations"

According to James C.Van Horne and Jhon M.Wachowicz, "financial management is considered with acquisition, financing and management of assets with some overall goal in mind".

According to Howard, "financial management involves the application of general management principles to a particular financial operation"

1.5. Objectives of the Financial Management

To make wise decisions a clear understanding of the objectives which are sought to be achieved is necessary. The objective provides a framework for optimum financial decision making. In other words, they are concerned with designing a method of operating the internal investment and financing of the firm. The term 'objective' is used in the sense of a goal or decision criterion for the three decisions involved in financial management. It implies that what is relevant is not the overall objective or goal of a business but a operationally useful criterion by which to judge a specific set of mutually interrelated business decisions, namely, investment, financing and dividend policy. Moreover, it provides a normative framework. The implication is that these are not necessarily followed by firms in actual practice. They are rather employed to serve as a basis for theoretical analysis and do not reflect contemporary empirical industry practices. Thus, the term is used in a rather narrow sense of what a firm should attempt to achieve with its investment, financing and dividend policy decisions.

The main objective of a business is tom maximize the owner's economic welfare. Financial management provides a framework for selecting a proper course of action and deciding a commercial strategy. The objectives can be achieved by: (i) Profit maximization (ii) Wealth maximization

Profit Maximization: Profit earning is the main aim of every economic activity. A business being an economic institution must earn profit to cover its cists and provide funds for growth. No business ca survives without earning profit. Profit is a measure of efficiency of a business enterprise. Profit also serves as a protection against risks which cannot be ensured.

Arguments in Favor of Profit Maximization

1. When profit earning is the aim of the business then the profit maximization should be the obvious objective.
2. Profitability is the barometer for measuring the efficiency and economic prosperity of a business enterprise, thus profit maximization is justified on the ground of the rationality.
3. Profits are the main source of finance for the growth of the business. So a business should aim at maximization of the profits for enabling its growth and development.
4. Profitability is essential for fulfilling the social goals also. A firm by pursuing the objectives of profits maximization also maximizes the socio economic welfare.
5. A business may be able to survive under unfavorable condition only if it had some past earnings to rely upon.

Arguments Against of Profit Maximization

1. It is precisely defined. It means different things for different people. The term 'Profit' is vague and it cannot be precisely defined. It means different things for different people. Should we mean (i) Short term profit or long term profit? (ii) Total profit or earning per share? (iii) Profit before tax or after tax? (iv) Operating profit or profit available for the shareholders?
2. It ignores the time value of money and does not consider the magnitude and the timing of earnings. It treats all the earnings as equal though they occur in different

time periods. It ignores the fact that the cash received today is more important than the same amount if cash received after, say, three years.

3. It does not take into consideration the risk of the prospective earning stream. Some projects are more risky than others. Two firms may have same expected earnings per share, but if the earning stream in one is more risky the market share of its share will be comparatively less.
4. The effect of the dividend policy on the market price of the shares is also not considered in the objective of the profit maximization. In case, earnings per share is the only objective then the enterprise may not think of paying dividends at all because it retains profits in the business or investing them in the market may satisfy this aim.

Wealth Maximization: Financial theory asserts that the wealth maximization is the single substitute for a stake holder's utility. When the firm maximizes the shareholder's wealth, the individual stakeholders can use this wealth to maximize his individual utility. It means that by maximizing stakeholder's wealth the firm is operating consistently toward maximizing stakeholder's utility.

A stake solder's wealth in the firm is the product of the numbers of the shares owned, multiplied within the current stock price per share.

Stockholder's current wealth in the firm = (No. Of shares owned) * (Current stock price per share)

Higher the stock price per share, the greater will be the shareholder's wealth. Thus a firm should aim at maximizing its current stock price, which helps in increasing the value of shares in the Market.

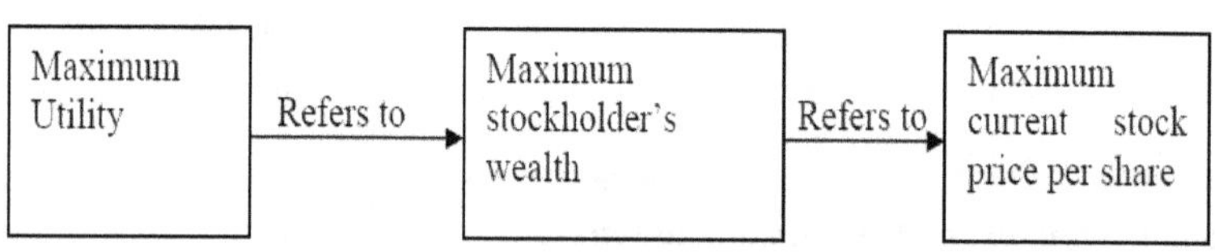

Implication of the Wealth Maximization

1. The Concept of wealth maximization is universally accepted, because it takes care of interest of financial institution, owners, employees and society at large.
2. Wealth maximization guides the management in framing the consistent strong dividend policy to reach maximum returns to the equity holders.

3. Wealth maximization objective not only serves the interest of the shareholder's by increasing the value of their holdings but also ensures the security to the lenders.

Criticism of Wealth Maximization

1. It is a prescriptive idea. The objective is not descriptive of what the firm actually does.
2. The objective of wealth maximization is not necessarily socially desirable.
3. There is some controversy as to whether the objective is to maximize the stockholder's wealth or the wealth of the firm, which includes other financial claimholder's such as debenture holders, preference shareholders.
4. The objective of wealth maximization may also face difficulties when ownership and management are separated, as is the case in most of the corporate form of organizations. When managers act as the agents of the real owner, there is the possibility for a conflict of interest between shareholders and the managerial interests.

1.6. Financial Decisions

Finance may be defined as the art and science of managing money. The major areas of finance are: (1) financial services and (2) managerial finance/corporate finance/ financial management.

While financial services is concerned within the areas of banking and related institutions, personal financial planning, investments, real estate, insurance and so on, financial management is concerned with the duties of the financial managers in the business firm.

Financial managers actively manage the financial affairs of any type of business, namely, financial and non-financial, private and public, large and small, profit seeking and not-for-profit. They perform such varied tasks as budgeting, financial forecasting, cash management, credit administration, investment analysis, funds management and so on.

Financial Management is the application of the general management principles in the area of financial decision-making, namely in the areas of investment of funds, financing various activities, and disposal of profits.

Financial management is the art of planning; organizing, directing and controlling of the procurement and utilization of the funds and safe disposal of profits to the end that individual,

Organizational and social objectives are accomplished.

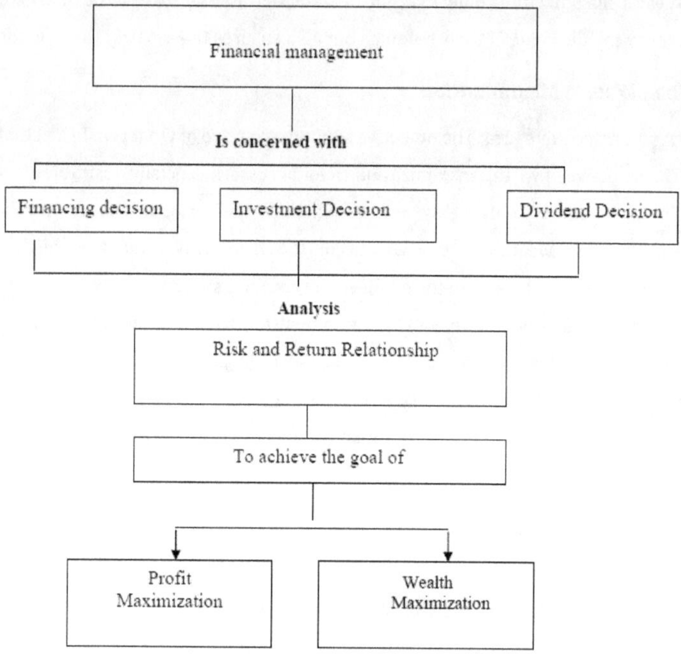

Financial Management Interrelationships

Financing Decision: The second major decision involved in financial management is the financing decision. The investment decision is broadly concerned with the asset-mix or the composition of the assets of a firm. The concern of the financing decision is with the financing mix or capital structure or leverage. The term capital structure refers to the proportion of debt (fixed interest sources of financing) and equity capital (variable-dividend securities/source of funds). The financing decision of a firm relates to the choice of the proposition of these sources to finance the investment requirements. A capital structure with a reasonable proportion of debt and equity capital is called the optimum capital structure.

Dividend Decision: The third major decision area of financial management is the decision relating to the dividend policy. The dividend decision should be analyzed in relation to the financing decision of a firm. Two alternatives are available in dealing with the profits of a firm: (i) they can be distributed to the shareholders in the form of dividends or (ii) they can be retained in the business itself. The decision as to which course should be followed depends largely on a significant element in the dividend decision, the dividend payout ratio, that is, what proportion of net profits should be paid out to the shareholders. The final decision will depend upon the preference of the shareholders and investment opportunities available within the firm. The second major aspect of the dividend decision is the factors determining dividend policy of a firm in practice.

1.7. Role of Finance Manager

A financial manager has to concentrate on the following areas of the finance function.

1. **Estimating Financial Requirements:** The first task of the financial manager is to estimate short term and long-term financial requirement of his business. For this purpose, he will prepare a financial plan for present as well as future. The amount required for purchasing fixed assets as well as the needs of funds for working capital has to be ascertained. The estimation should be based on the sound financial principles so that neither there are inadequate or excess funds with the concern. The inadequacy will affect the working of the concern and excess funds may tempt a management to indulge in extravagant spending.
2. **Deciding Capital Structure:** The capital structure refers to the kind and proportion of the different securities for raising funds. After deciding about the quantum of funds required it should be decided which type of security should be raised. It may be wise to finance fixed securities through long term debts. Long-term funds should be employed to finance working capital also. Decision about various sources of funds should be linked to cost of raising funds. If cost of rising funds is high, then such sources may not be useful. A decision about the kind of the securities to be employed and the proportion in which these should be used is an important decision which influences the short term and the long term planning of the enterprise.
3. **Selecting a Source of Finance:** After preparing a capital structure, an appropriate source of finance is selected. Various sources from which finance may be raised, includes share capital, debentures, financial deposits etc. If finance is needed for short periods then banks, public's deposits, financial institutions may be appropriate. If long-term finance is required the share capital, debentures may be useful.
4. **Selecting a Pattern of Investment:** When fund have been procured then a decision about investment pattern is to be taken. The selection of investment pattern is related to the use of the funds. A decision has to be taken as to which assets are to be purchased? The fund will have to be spent first. Fixed asset and the appropriate portion will be retained for the working capital. The decision making techniques such as capital Budgeting, opportunity cost analysis may be applied in making decision

about capital expenditures. While spending in various assets, the principles of safety, profitability, and liquidity should not be ignored.

5. **Proper Cash Management:** Cash management is an important task of financial manager. He has to assess the various cash needs at different times and then make arrangements for arranging cash. Cash may be required to make payments to creditors, purchasing raw material, meet wage bills, and meet day to day expenses. The sources of cash may be Cash sales, Collection of debts, Short-term arrangement with the banks. The cash management should be such that neither there is shortage of it and nor it is idle. Any shortage of cash will damage the creditworthiness of the enterprise. The idle cash with the business mean that it is nit properly used. Through Cash Flow Statement one is able to find out various sources and applications of cash.
6. **Implementing Financial Controls:** An efficient system of financial management necessitates the use of various control devices. Financial control device generally used are;
    - Return Investment
    - Ratio analysis
    - Break even analysis
    - Cost control
    - Cost and internal audit.
7. **The use of various control techniques:** This will help the financial manager in evaluating the performance in various Areas and take corrective measures whenever needed.
8. **Proper use of Surpluses:** The utilization of profits or surpluses as also an important factor in financial management. A judicious use of surpluses is essential for the expansion and diversification plans and also protecting the interest of the shareholders. The ploughing back of profit is the best policy of further financing. A balance should be struck in using the funds for paying dividends and retaining earnings for financing expansion plans.

1.8. Time Value of Money

1.8.1. Introduction

Time value of money means that the value of unit of money is different in different time periods. The value of a sum of money received today is more than its value received after some time. Conversely, the sum of money received in future is less valuable than it is today. In other words, the present worth of a rupee received after some time will be less than a rupee received today. Since a rupee received today has more value, rational investors would prefer current receipt to future receipts. The time value of money can also be referred to as time preference for money.

Most financial decisions, such as the purchase of assets or procurement of funds, affect the firm's cash flows in different time periods. For example, if fixed asset are purchased it will require immediate cash outlays sand will generate cash flows during many future periods. Similarly, if firm borrows funds from the bank it receives cash now and commits an obligation to pay interest and repay principal in future periods. Cash flows become logically comparable when they are appropriately adjusted for their differences in time and risk.

The recognition of the time value of money and risk is extremely vital in financial decision making. If the timing and risk of cash flows is not considered, the firm may make decision, which may allow too its objectives of maximize the owner's welfare. The welfare of the owners would be maximized when net worth or net value is created from making a financial decision.

Concept of Time Value of Money

- Valuation of financial securities
- Valuation of firms
- Valuation of capital budgeting, merger and acquisition
- Personal finance
- Leasing and hire purchase transactions.

Reasons for Individual's Time Preference for Money

a. Uncertainty: An individual is not certain about future cash receipts, he prefers receiving cash now.

b. Preference for Consumption: Most people have subjective preference for present consumption over future consumption of goods and services either because of the urgency of their present wants or because of the risk of not being in a position to enjoy future consumption that may be caused by illness or death. As money is the means by which individuals acquire most goods and services, they may prefer to money have now.

c. Investment Opportunities: Most individuals prefer present cash to future cash because of the available opportunities to which they can put present cash to earn additional cash. For e.g., an individual who is offered Rs. 100 now or Rs 100 one year from now would prefer Rs100 now if he could earn interest of Rs 5 by putting in the saving account in the bank for one year. His total cash in one year from now will be Rs.105.

1.8.2. *Techniques*

- Compounding technique
- Present value or discounting technique

Compounding Technique

Interest is compounded when the amount earned on an initial deposit becomes part of the principal at the end of the first compounding period. The term principal refers to the amount of money on which interest is received. This compounding procedure will continue for an indefinite number of years. The compounding interest can be calculated by the following equation:

$$A=P\,(1+i)^{n}$$

in which

A= amount at the end of the period

P= principal at the beginning of the period

i= rate of interest

n= number of years

Types of Compounding

Semi-annual compounding: means two compounding periods within a year.

Quarterly compounding: means four compounding periods in a year

Annuity: is a stream of equal annual cash flows.

Present Value or Discounting Technique

The concept of the present value is the exact opposite of that of compound value. While in the latter approach money invested now appreciates in value because compound interest is added, in the former approach (present value approach) money is received at some future date and will be worth less because the corresponding interest is lost during the period. In other words, the present value of a rupee that will be received in the future will be less than the value of a rupee in hand today. Thus, in contrast to the compounding approach where we convert the present sums into future sums, in present value approach future sums are converted into present sums. Given a positive rate of interest, the present value of future rupees will always be lower. It is for this reason, therefore, that the procedure of finding present values is commonly called discounting. It is concerned with determining the present value of a future amount, assuming that the decision maker has an opportunity to earn a certain return on his money.

Present value equation:

$$P = \frac{A}{(1+i)^n}$$

$$A\{1/(1+i)^n\}$$

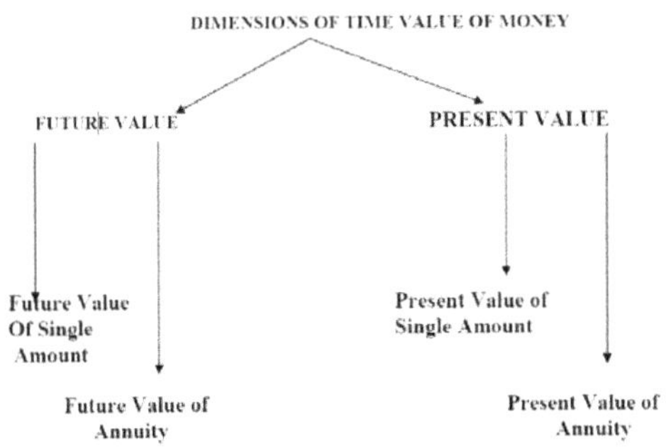

Future Value of a Single Amount: Suppose you have Rs. 1000 today and you deposit it with a financial institution, which pays 10% interest compound annually, for a period of 2 years.

		Rs.
Ist Year	Principal at the beginning	1000
	Interest for the year	100
	Principal at the end	1100
IInd Year	Principal at the beginning	1100
	Interest for the year	110
	Principal at the end	1210

Formula

$$FV_n = PV\,(1+k)^n$$

Where FV_n = future value n years hence

PV = present value

k = interest rate per year

n = number of year for which compounding is done.

The factor (1+k) n is referred to as the compounding factor or the Future Value Interest Factor (FVIFk,n)

Illustration 1

If you deposit Rs. 1000 today in a bank which pays 10% interest compounded annually, how much will the deposit grow to after 8 years and 12 years?

Rs. 1000(1.10) 8 = Rs. 1000(2.144) = Rs. 2.144

The future value, 12 years hence will be:

Rs. 1000(1.10) 12 = Rs. 1000(3.318) = Rs. 3.318

$$FV_n = PV \left(1 + \frac{k}{m}\right)^{m*n}$$

Where FV_n = future value after n years

PV = cash flow today

k = nominal annual rate of interest

m= number of times computing

n = number of years

Future Value of Annuity: An annuity is a series of periodic cash flows (payments or receipts) of equal amounts. The premium payment of a life insurance policy, for example, is an annuity.

Illustration 2: Coca-Cola Enterprises Borrows Some Cash

In 1995 Coca-Cola Enterprises needed to borrow about a quarter of a billion dollars for 25 years. It did so by selling IOUs, each of which simply promised to pay the holder $1,000 at the end of 25 years.1 The market interest rate at the time was 8.53 percent. How much would you have been prepared to pay for one of the company's IOUs?

To calculate present value we multiply the $1,000 future payment by the 25-year discount factor:

PV = $1,000 × 1

(1.0853)25

= $1,000 × .129 = $129

Illustration 3

Suppose you deposit Rs 1000 annually in a bank for 5 year and your deposits

Earn a compound interest rate of 10%. What will be the value of series of deposits at the end of 5 years?

Rs 1000(1.10) 4 + Rs 1000(1.10) 3 + Rs1000 (1.10) 2 + Rs 1000(1.10) 2 + 1000 (1.10)

=Rs 6105

$$FVAn = A \left[\frac{(1+k)\,n \;\; - 1}{K} \right]$$

Where FVAn = future value of an annuity which has a duration of n Period

A = Constant periodic flow

K = Interest rate per period

N – Duration of the annuity

The term $\frac{(1+k)\,n\,-\,1}{K}$ is referred to as the **future value interest factor for an annuity.**

i.e. (FVIFAn)

Present Value of a Single Amount: The present value of a future cash inflows or outflow is the amount of current cash flow that is equivalent desirability, to the decision maker, to a specified amount of cash to be received or paid at the future date. The process of determining the present value of a future payment or a series of future payments is called discounting.

Illustration 4

Suppose someone gives you Rs1000 six year hence. What is the present value of this amount if the interest rate is 10%?

Formula:

$$PV = FVn \left[\frac{1}{1+k} \right]^n$$

The factor $\left[\frac{1}{1+k} \right]^n$ Is called the discounting factor or **(PVIFkn)**

The present value is

Rs1000 (PVIF10%, 6) = Rs 1000 (0.5645) = 564.5

Illustration 5

Find the present value of Rs1000 receivable 20 years hence if the discount rate is 8%.

$$Rs1000 \left(\frac{1}{1.08}\right)^{20} = Rs1000 \left(\frac{1}{1.08}\right)^{10} \left(\frac{1}{1.08}\right)^{10}$$

$$= Rs1000\ (PVIF8\%, 10)\ (PVIF8\%, 10)$$
$$1000(0.463)\ (0.463) = Rs214$$

= Rs1000 (PVIF8%, 10) (PVIF8%, 10)

1000(0.463) (0.463) = Rs214

Present Value of an Annuity

$$PVAn = A \left(\frac{(1+k)n - 1}{K(1+k)n}\right)$$

PVAn = Present value of annuity having duration n periods

A = constant periodic flow

K = Discount Rate

Illustration 6

Present value of a 4 year annuity of Rs10000 discounted at 10%

PVA4 = 10000(PVIFA10%,4) = 10000(3.170) = 31700

1.9. Valuation of Bonds and Shares

1.9.1. Introduction

Valuation is the process that links risk and return to determine the worth of an asset. It can be applied to expected benefits from real/physical as well as financial to determine their worth at a given point of time. We will focus on valuation of two financial assets, namely, bonds/debentures and shares. .the key inputs to valuation process are i) expected returns in terms of cash flows together with their timing and ii) risk in terms of the required return.

The value of an asset depends on the return (cash flow) it is expected to provide over the holding /ownership period. The cash flow stream can be (1) annual, (2) intermittent and (3) even onetime.

In addition to total cash flow estimates, their timing/pattern (e.g. amount year-wise) is also required to identify the return expected from the bond/share. The required return is used in the valuation process to incorporate risk into the analysis. Risk denotes the chance that an expected cash flow would not be realized. The level of risk associated with a expected cash flow/return has a significant bearing on its value, that is, the greater the risk, the lower the value and *vice versa.* Higher risk can be incorporated into the valuation analysis by using a higher capitalization/ discount rate to determine the present value.

Valuation of securities will be discussed in following parts:

1. The basic valuation model
2. Valuation of Bond / Debenture
   a. Basic bond valuation
   b. Yield to maturity
   c. Semi-annual interest and bond value
3. Valuation of preference shares
4. Valuation of ordinary shares
   a. Zero growth model
   b. Constant growth model / Gordon model
   c. Variable growth model

The Basic Valuation Model: The value of an security is the present value of all future cash flows associated with it over the specified period. The expected returns are discounted, using the required return matching with the risk of asset as the appropriate discount rate. Symbolically,

$$V = \frac{A_1}{(1+k)^1} + \frac{A_2}{(1+k)^2} + \cdots + \frac{A_n}{(1+k)^n}$$

Where V = Value of security at time zero (t = 0)

At = cash flow stream expected at the end of year t

K = appropriate discount rate

Alternatively, where Expected Cash Flows is a Mixed Stream

V = [(A1 x PVIFk,1) + (A2 x PVIFk,2) +- - - - - + (An x PVIFk,n)

Where'

PVIF1, PVIF2, PVIFn = present value interest factor in different period at discount rate k.

If expected cash flow is an Annuity, V = A * PVIFA (k,n)

Illustration 7

Assuming a discount rate of 10 percent, and the associated cash flows detailed below. Compute the value of assets X and Y.

Year	Expected cash flow	
	X	Y
1	Rs.10,000	5,000
2	10,000	10,000
3	10,000	15,000

Solution

Value of asset X = Rs 10,000 x PVIFA (10,3) = Rs 10,000 x 2.4870 = Rs.24,870

Value of asset Y: = [(Rs.5, 000 x PVIF10,1) + (Rs. 10,000 xPVIF10,,2) + (Rs. 15,000 x PVIF10,3)

= [(Rs.5, 000 x 0.909) + (Rs. 10,000 x 0.826) + (Rs. 15,000 x 0.751)

= Rs.4545+ RS.8260+Rs.11265 = Rs. 24,070

1.9.2. Valuation of Bonds/Debentures

A bond / debenture are a long term debt instrument used by the government/ business/ enterprises to raise a large sum of money. Most bonds (i) pay interest half yearly at a stated coupon interest rate, (ii) have a maturity of 10-years and (iii) have a par/face value of Rs 1,000 that must be repaid at maturity. **Par value** is the value on the face of the bond. It represents the amount the entity borrows and promises to repay at the time of maturity. **Coupon is** the specified interest rate. The interest payable to the bondholder is equal to par value x coupon rate. **Maturity period** refers to the number of years after which the par value is payable to the bondholder.

A Basic Bond Valuation: The value of bond is the present value of the contractual payments its issuer is obliged .to make from the beginning till maturity.. The appropriate discount rate would be the required return matching with risk and the prevailing interest rate. Symbolically,

$$B = \mathrm{I}\left[\sum_{t=1}^{n} \frac{1}{(1+k_d)^t}\right] + M * \left[\frac{1}{(1+k_d)^n}\right] \quad = \mathrm{I} \times (\mathrm{PVIF}A_{k_d n}) + \mathrm{M} \times (\mathrm{PVI}F_{k_d n})$$

Where

B = value of the bond at $t = 0$

I = annual interest paid

n = number of years' to maturity (term of the bond)

M = Par/maturity value

k_d= required return on the bond

Impact of Maturity on Bond Value: When the required return (RR) is different from rate of interest (CR), the time to maturity would affect value of bonds even though RR remains constant till maturity. The relationship among (i) time to maturity, (ii) the RR and (iii) value are related to (a) constant RR and (b) changing RR.

Constant Required Returns: In such a situation the value of the bond would approach as the passage of time moves the value of the bond closer to maturity.

Changing Required Returns: The shorter the time period until a bond's maturity, the less responsive is its market value to a given change in the required return. In other words, short maturities have less "interest rate risk" than do long maturities when all other features, namely, CR, par value, frequency of interest payment, are the same.

For example taking the same facts as in illustration 2 and 3, each of the three required returns (i.e. 12, 10, and 8) is assumed to remain constant over the 10 years to its maturity. In each case, the value ultimately equals the par value of maturity. At the 12 per cent RR, its discount declines with the passage of time as its value increases from Rs 887 to Rs 1,000. When the 10 per cent RR equals the CR, its value remains Rs 1,000. Finally, at the 8 per cent RR, its premium will decline as its value drops fro Rs 1,000. Thus, the value of a bond approaches Rs 1,000 Par/maturity value as the time to maturity declines.

Yield to Maturity: The **YTM** is the rate of return that investors earn if they buy a bond at a specific price and hold it until maturity. It assumes that the issuer of the bond makes all due interest payment and repayments of principal as contracted/promised. The YTM on a bond whose price equals its par/face value (i.e. purchase price = maturity value) would always be equal to its coupon interest rate. In case the bond value differs from the par value the YTM would differ from the CR.

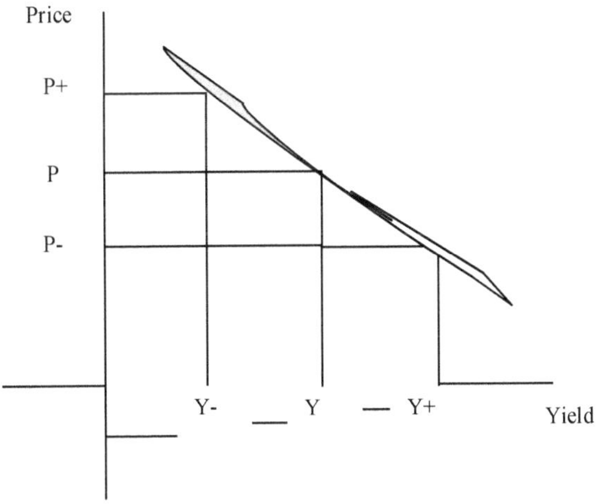

Relationship between YTM and Bond Price

1.10. Definition of Return & Risk

1.10.1. Introduction

Return: The (rate of) return of an asset/investment for a given period, say a year, is the annual income received plus any change in market price, usually expressed as a percent of the opening market price. Symbolically, the one period actual(expected) return

$$R = \frac{D_t + (P_t - P_{t-1})}{P_{t-1}}$$

Risk: The variability of the actual return from the expected returns associated with a given asset/investment is defined as risk. The greater the variability, the riskier the security (eg. shares) is said to be. The more certain the return from an asset (eg. T.bills), the less the variability and, therefore, the less the risk.

Measurement of Risk: The risk associated with a single asset is assessed from both a behavioral and a quantitative/ statistical point of view. The behavioral view of risk can be obtained by using (i) Sensitivity analysis and (ii) probability (distribution). The statistical measures of risk of an asset/security are (1) Standard deviation and (2) coefficient of variation.

Sensitivity analysis takes into account a number of possible outcomes/returns estimates while evaluating an asset/assessing risk. In order to have a sense of the variability among return estimates, a possible approach is to estimate the worst (pessimistic), the expected (most likely) and the best (optimistic) return associated with the asset.

Probability (distribution) The risk associated with an asset can be assessed more accurately by the use of probability (distribution) than sensitivity analysis. The probability of an event represents the likelihood/percentage change of its occurrence.

1.10.2. Types of Risk

Systematic Risk

- Market risk
- Interest rate risk
- Purchasing power risk

Unsystematic Risk

- Business risk
- Financial risk

1. Market Risk

The risk of investments declining in value because of economic developments or other events that affect the entire market. The main types of market risk are equity risk, interest rate risk and currency risk.

Equity risk - applies to an investment in shares. The market price of shares varies all the time depending on demand and supply. Equity risk is the risk of loss because of a drop in the market price of shares.

Interest rate risk - applies to debt investments such as bonds. It is the risk of losing money because of a change in the interest rate. For example, if the interest rate goes up, the market value of bonds will drop.

Currency risk - applies when you own foreign investments. It is the risk of losing money because of a movement in the exchange rate. For example, if the U.S. dollar becomes less valuable relative to the Canadian dollar, your U.S. stocks will be worth less in Canadian dollars.

2. Liquidity Risk

The risk of being unable to sell your investment at a fair price and get your money out when you want to. To sell the investment, you may need to accept a lower price. In some cases, such as exempt market investments, it may not be possible to sell the investment at all.

3. Concentration Risk

The risk of loss because your money is concentrated in 1 investment or type of investment. When you diversify your investments, you spread the risk over different types of investments, industries and geographic locations.

4. Credit Risk

The risk that the government entity or company that issued the bond will run into financial difficulties and won't be able to pay the interest or repay the principal at maturity. Credit risk applies to debt investments such as bonds. You can evaluate credit risk by looking at the credit rating of the bond. For example, long-term Canadian government bonds have a credit rating of AAA, which indicates the lowest possible credit risk.

5. Reinvestment Risk

The risk of loss from reinvesting principal or income at a lower interest rate. Suppose you buy a bond paying 5%. Reinvestment risk will affect you if interest rates drop and you have to reinvest the regular interest payments at 4%. Reinvestment risk will also apply if the bond matures and you have to reinvest the principal at less than 5%. Reinvestment risk will not apply if you intend to spend the regular interest payments or the principal at maturity.

6. Inflation Risk

The risk of a loss in your purchasing power because the value of your investments does not keep up with inflation. Inflation erodes the purchasing power of money over time – the same amount of money will buy fewer goods and services. Inflation risk is particularly relevant if you own cash or debt investments like bonds. Shares offer some protection against inflation because most companies can increase the prices they charge to their customers. Share prices should therefore rise in line with inflation. Real estate also offers some protection because landlords can increase rents over time.

7. Horizon Risk

The risk that your investment horizon may be shortened because of an unforeseen event, for example, the loss of your job. This may force you to sell investments that you were expecting to hold for the long term. If you must sell at a time when the markets are down, you may lose money.

8. Longevity Risk

The risk of outliving your savings. This risk is particularly relevant for people who are retired, or are nearing retirement.

9. Foreign Investment Risk

The risk of loss when investing in foreign countries. When you buy foreign investments, for example, the shares of companies in emerging markets, you face risks that do not exist in Canada, for example, the risk of nationalization.

1.10.3. Risk and Return of a Single Asset

The expected return on an asset can be divided into two parts: i) the return for deferring consumption, and ii) a compensation for bearing risk. The return for deferring compensation is, of course, simply rf, the return on the risk-free asset. Hence the return for bearing risk is E(ri) - rf. Mean-variance analysis implies that the return for bearing risk is proportional to the risk. Consequently, we can write the risk-return relationship as:

$$E(ri) - rf = bi\ [E(rm) - rf]$$

where the constant of proportionality is naturally the risk premium on the market portfolio, which has a beta of unity.

This equilibrium relationship has several desirable features:

The expected return on a security with a beta of zero is equal to the riskfree rate, rf. Since such a security contributes nothing to the (market) portfolio risk, it is effectively riskless (even though its return variance may be positive).

An asset with a beta of one is equivalent to the market portfolio and earns the expected rate of return on the market portfolio.

If two assets are priced to satisfy the above risk-return pricing equation, then so will their combination.

1.10.4. Risk and Return of Portfolio

A portfolio means a combination of two or more securities (assets). A large number of portfolios can be formed from a given set of assets. Each portfolio has risk-return characteristics of its own. Portfolio theory, originally developed by Harry Markowitz, shows that portfolio risk, unlike portfolio return, is more than a simple aggregation of the risk of individual assets. This depends on the interplay between the returns on assets comprising the portfolio. As investors construct a portfolio of investment rather than invest in a single asset.

Portfolio Expected Return

The expected rate of return on a portfolio is the weighted average of the expected rates of return on assets comprising the portfolio. The weights, which add up to 1, reflect the fraction of total portfolio invested in each asset. Thus, there are two determinants of portfolio return: expected rate of return on each asset and the relative share of each asset in the portfolio. Symbolically, the expected return for a n-asset portfolio is defined by:

$$E(r_p) = \sum w_i \, E(r_i)$$

Where $E(r_p)$= Expected return from portfolio

w_i= Proportion invested in asset i

$E(r_i)$= Expected return for asset i

n= Number of assets in portfolio

MINICASE

Old Alfred Road, who is well-known to drivers on the Maine Turnpike, has reached his seventieth birthday and is ready to retire. Mr. Road has no formal training in finance but has saved his money and invested carefully. Mr. Road owns his home-the mortgage is paid off-and does not want to move. He is a widower, and he wants to bequeath the house and any remaining assets to his daughter. He has accumulated savings of $180,000, conservatively invested. The investments are yielding 9 percent interest. Mr. Road also has $12,000 in a savings account at 5 percent interest. He wants to keep the savings account intact for unexpected expenses or emergencies. Mr. Road's basic living expenses now average about $1,500 per month, and he plans to spend $500 per month on travel and hobbies. To maintain this planned standard of living, he will have to rely on his investment portfolio. The interest from the portfolio is $16,200 per year (9 percent of $180,000), or $1,350 per month. Mr. Road will also receive $750 per month in social security payments for the rest of his life. These payments are indexed for inflation. That is, they will be automatically increased in proportion to changes in the consumer price index. Mr. Road's main concern is with inflation. The inflation rate has been below 3 percent recently, but a 3 percent rate is unusually low by historical standards. His social security payments will increase with inflation, but the interest on his investment portfolio will not. What advice do you have for Mr. Road? Can he safely spend all the interest from his investment portfolio? How much could he withdraw at year-end from that portfolio if he wants to keep its real value intact? Suppose Mr. Road will live for 20 more years and is willing to use up his entire investment portfolio over that period. He also wants his monthly spending to increase along with inflation over that period. In other words, he wants his monthly spending to stay the same in real terms. How much can he afford to spend per month?

Assume that the investment portfolio continues to yield a 9 percent rate of return and that the inflation rate is 4 percent.

Review Questions

1. Define finance. Explain the concept of finance.
2. Explain the nature of financial management.
3. Describe the significance of financial management.
4. Explain the functions of financial management.
5. Explain the risk and returns.
6. What is unsystematic risk? Explain.
7. What are the reasons for time value of money?
8. What is time value of money? Explain the concept of time value of money.
9. Evaluate the goals of financial management.
10. Suppose you have Rs.30,000 today and deposit it with a financial institution, which pays 15% interest compounded annually, for a period of 4 years. Find the future value of deposit.
11. Suppose you deposit Rs.5,000 with a finance company which advertises that it pays 12% interest semi annually (ie interest is paid every six months). Find the future value.
12. You have Rs.1,00,000 available today for investment. A bank has offered 10% interest payable annually. For how long you invest with the bank so that the amount is doubled? How much would be the simple interest for this period?
13. XYZ Ltd. registered sales of Rs.200 lakhs in the year 2005. If the sales are growing at 15% annually, what is the projected turnover of XYZ Ltd. After 10 years?
14. Suppose you decide to deposit Rs.1000 annually for 5 years at 8% in a bank. What is the maturity amount at the end of five years?
15. Suppose you have Rs.27000 today and needed to preserve it for the next 8 years when you are required to pay fees for your son. Which estimated to be Rs.90,000?
    a. At what rate should you invest this money so as to have the required sum at the end of 8 years?
    b. If you needed Rs.90,000 after 8 years at 12% what amount should you invest today?

CHAPTER 2

INVESTMENT DECISIONS

2.1. Capital Budgeting

2.1.1. *Definition*

Capital budgeting is long-term planning for making and financing proposed capital outlays. -Charles T. Horngreen.

The capital budgeting generally refers to acquiring inputs with long-returns. - Richards and Greenlaw.

Capital Budgeting is known as investment decision making, capital expenditure decision, planning capital expenditure and analysis of capital expenditure.

Capital Budgeting/Capital Expenditure Budget

Capital budgeting is a process of making decisions regarding investments in fixed assets which are not meant for sale such as machinery, plant, building etc., and the benefits of which are expected to be received over a number of years in future.

Features of Capital Budgeting

- It has the potentiality of making large anticipated profits.
- It involves a high degree of risk.
- It involves a relatively long time period between the initial outlay and anticipated return.
- The future benefits are expected to be realized over a series of years.
- They involve, generally, huge funds.
- They are irreversible decisions.
- They have a long term and significant effect on the profitability of the concern
- Capital budgeting decision involves the exchange of current funds for the benefits to be achieved in future.

2.1.2. *Objectives of Capital Expenditure Budget*

- It determines the capital projects on the basis of its urgency and the expected rate of return.
- It determines the expected rate of return on each project.

- It estimates the expenditure that would have to be incurred on capital projects approved by the management together with the sources from which the required funds would be obtained.
- To coordinate inter departmental projects.
- To measure the performance of on-going projects.
- To prevent cost over-runs on the projects.

2.1.3. Importance/ Signification of Capital Budgeting

- Involvement of heavy funds
- Long-term implications
- Irreversible decision
- Most difficult to make
- Cost over runs
- Alternatives
- Multiplicity of variables
- Top Management activities
- Large investments
- Long-term effect on profitability
- Maximization of shareholders wealth
- National importance
- Difficulties of investment decision

2.1.4. Need for Capital Budgeting

- Analyse the proposal for expansion or creating additional capacities.
- To decide the replacement of permanent assets such as building and equipments.
- To make financial analysis of various proposals regarding capital investments so as to choose the best out of many alternative proposals.
- Whether or not funds should be invested in long-term projects such as setting of industry, purchase of plant and machinery, etc.

2.1.5. Process of Capital Budgeting Appraisal Method

- A basis of distinguishing between acceptable and non-acceptable projects.
- Ranking of projects in order of their desirability.
- Choosing among several alternatives.
- Criterion which is applicable to any conceivable project.

- Recognising the fact that bigger benefits are preferable to smaller ones and early benefits are preferable to later ones.

Nature of Capital budgeting

- Capital plans involve a huge investment in fixed assets.
- Capital expenditure once approved represents long-term investment that cannot be withdrawn without sustaining a loss.
- Preparation of capital budget plans involves forecasting of projects.
- Any error in the evaluation of investment projects may lead to serious consequences, financially and otherwise and may adversely affect the other future plans of the organization.

Important Steps in the Capital Budgeting Process

- Identification of investment proposals
- Screening the proposals
- Evaluation of various proposals
- Fixing priorities
- Implementing proposal
- Performance review

Factors Considered While Estimating the Future Cash Flows

While estimating the future cash flows the following should be considered:

- Expected economic life of the project
- Salvage value of the asset at the end of the economic life
- Capacity of the project
- Selling price of the product
- Production cost
- Depreciation rate
- Rate of taxation
- Future demand of the product etc.

2.1.6. Factors Affecting Capital Investment Decision

- Urgency:

Sometimes an investment is to be made due to urgency for the survival of the firm or to avoid heavy losses.

E.g.: break down of some plant, machinery, fire, accident etc.

1. *Intangible Factors*

Sometimes a capital expenditure has to be made due to certain emotional and intangible factors such as safety and welfare of workers, prestigious projects, social welfare, goodwill of the firm etc.,

2. *Legal Factors*

An investment which is required by the provisions of law is solely influenced by this factor and although the project may not be profitable the investment has to be made.

3. *Availability of Funds*

As the capital expenditure, generally, requires large funds, the availability of funds is an important factor that influences the capital budgeting decisions. The high yielding projects are sometimes rejected simply because the required funds for them cannot be arranged. If adequate funds are not available, a project having lower payback period is preferred despite its low profitability.

4. *Future Earnings*

If management has plans for undertaking more profitable projects in future, it may at present choose those investment proposals whose economic life or payback period is very short, although they may be less remunerative.

5. *Risk and Uncertainty*

Different capital investment proposals have different degrees of risk and uncertainty. The risk involves situations in which the probabilities of occurrence of a particular event are known and incase of uncertainty these probabilities are not known. Risk in capital investment decision may be due to changes in economic conditions, competitions, technological developments, labour conditions, consumer preferences, etc. Thus, it is an important factor the management has to consider while taking investment decisions.

6. *Obsolescence*

The risk of obsolescence is another important factor to be considered rather than profitability which affects the managerial decisions in respect of investment proposals.

7. *Cost Considerations*

Cost of capital of the project, cost of working capital, opportunity cost of capital etc are other considerations involved in the capital budgeting decisions.

Cut-off Point

Cut-off point refers to the point below which a project would not be accepted. The cut-off point is fixed on the basis of cost of capital. Therefore, the cut-off rate is also known as cost of capital.

The cut-off rates can be decided by using the following alternative methods:

- Weighted average cost of capital.
- Cost of funds to finance the expenditure.
- Historical rate of return and
- Arbitrary cut-off point established by management.

Moreover, the determination of cut-off rate varies widely between companies. A large number of industrial enterprises are still using the cut-off rate arbitrarily established by the management. Some high profitability companies employ cost of funds used to finance expenditure as cut-off rate. But, on the whole, the weighted average cost of capital is realized as a theoretically correct method for deciding the cut-off rate.

2.1.7. Methods of Appraisal

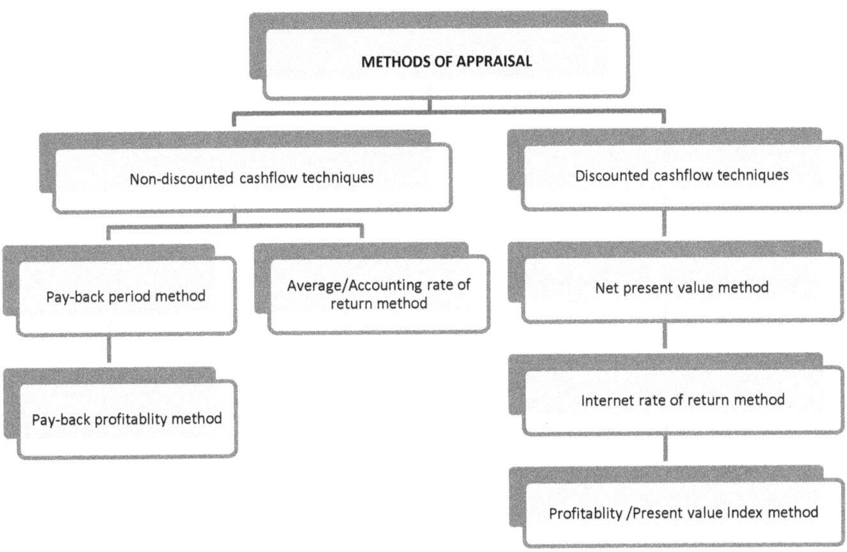

A. Traditional methods

- Urgency
- Pay-back period method

B. Accounting Rate of Return method or Average Rate of Return method

C. Discounted cash flow methods

- The Net present value method. (NPV)
- Present value index Method. (PI)
- Internal rate of Return Method (IRR)
- Discounted Pay-back Method.

Urgency Method

Virtually it is not a method of evaluation of project. Urgency plays an important role under this method. Hence, the project which is the most urgent and cannot be postponed is undertaken first in order to avoid disruption in the working.

Advantages

- This method is very simple on principle and practice
- No technique is needed.

Disadvantages

- No methodical analysis is applied.
- Role of persuasion of various departmental heads are possible.

Pay – back Method

Pay – back method is also called pay-off or pay-out method. It represents the number of years required to recover the original investments by savings before depreciation but after the payment of taxes.

Thus it attempts to measure the period of time it takes to recover the original cost of a project.

Computation of pay – back period:

- If the annual net cash – inflows are even

$$Pay-back\ period = \frac{\text{Original Investment}}{\text{Annual cash inflow}}$$

- If the annual net cash inflows are inflows are uneven, calculate the cumulate cash inflow and find out the number of years required to recover the original investment.

I.e.

$$Pay-back\ period = \frac{\text{Investment}}{\text{Cash inflows}}$$

Accept / Reject criterion: Project with shorter payback period is accepted.

Advantages

- It is easy to calculate and simple to understand
- The short-term approach typified by the payback method reduces the possibility of loss through obsolescence.
- It is preferred on the ground that returns beyond three or four years are so uncertain as to disregard them altogether in a planning decision.
- Built-in features.
- Profit is determined
- It acts guideline for dividend policy
- Importance to liquidity
- Manage with lower funds
- It saves cost.

Disadvantages

- It completely ignores the annual cash inflows after the payback period.
- It does not take into account the time value of the money.
- It ignores the interest which is an important factor in making sound investment decision.
- It is not concerned with the length of a project.
- Cash inflows are not recognized.
- It does not make to use of cost of capital.
- It is difficult to understand.
- It is a subjective decision.
- Investment in different assets is interrelated.
- It does not calculate the profitability of the projects.
- It is concerned with a short period of a project's life time

Developments in Traditional Approach to Pay-back Method

- Pay-back profitability method

$$= Total\ cash\ inflow - (Pay - back\ cash\ inflows)$$

- Post pay-back method (positive cash inflows)
- Pay-back reciprocal method or unadjusted rate of return method

$$= \frac{\text{Annual cash inflow}}{\text{Investment}} \text{ x } 100$$

Average Rate of Return method (ARR)

Average Rate of Return method is also known as Accounting Rate of Return method. Under this method the capital investment proposals are judged on the basis of their relative profitability.

It can be determined by the following formula:

$$ARR = \frac{\text{Annual Average Net Earning}}{\text{Original Investment (or) Average Investment}} \times 100$$

Calculation based on total income method can be determined as below,

$$ARR = \frac{\text{Total Earnings}}{\text{Original cost of investment} - \text{Scrap}} \times 100$$

Annual Average Net earnings = Earnings after depreciation and Tax.

$$\text{Average Investment} = \frac{\text{Original Investment}}{2}$$

Or

$$\frac{\text{Original Investment} - \text{Scrap value of the asset}}{2}$$

Or

$$\frac{\text{Original Investment} + \text{Scrap value of the asset}}{2}$$

Or

$$\frac{\left\{\begin{matrix}\text{Original}\\ \text{Investment}\end{matrix}\right\} - \text{Scrap value of the asset} + \left\{\begin{matrix}\text{Additional net}\\ \text{working capital}\end{matrix}\right\} + \text{Scrap}}{2}$$

Accept / Reject Criterion

- Single project: If the ARR is more than minimum rate of return, it can be accepted.
- Several projects: Rank in the ascending or descending order of their rate of return. Projects below the minimum rate of return will be rejected.

Merits

- It is very simple to understand and use.
- The system gives due weightage to the profitability of the project if based on average rate of return.
- It takes investment and the total earning from the project during its life time into consideration.
- It is based on accounting profit which is readily available.
- It provides a more comprehensive comparative assessment of projects

Demerits

- It ignores the time-value of money which is an important factor in capital expenditure decisions.
- It ignores the length of the project lives.
- There are different methods for calculating the Accounting Rate of Return due to diverse concepts of investments as well as earnings.
- It uses accounting profits and not the cash inflows in appraising the investment projects.
- Reliability of ARR method is affected due to the various concept of investment.
- ARR method is not properly assessed.
- Investment is made in two or more installments.

2.1.8. Discounted Cash Flow Method

The discounted cash flow technique is an improvement on the pay-back period method. It takes into account both the interest factor as well as the return after the payback period.

The method involves three stages

- Calculation of cash flows
- Discounting the cash flows
- Aggregating of discounted cash inflows

In general DCF technique provides quantitative, systematic and reliable shape to the concept of time value of money.

There are two reasons for assigning higher value to earlier incomes. These reasons are like foundations for the concept of time value of money.

- Interest aspects
- Uncertainty aspects

$$\text{DCF} = \frac{1}{(1 + r)^n}$$

Net Present Value Method

This generally considered to be the best method for evaluating the capital investment proposals. It recognizes the time value of money and that cash flows arising at different period of time differ in value and are not comparable unless their equivalent present values are found the present value of these cash inflows and outflows are then calculated at the rate of return acceptable to the management. It is also called Excess Present Value Method or Net Gain Method.

Steps to calculate the NPV:

- Cash inflows and cash outflows are first worked out.
- Profit after tax but before depreciation represents cash inflow.
- Present value of cash inflow is calculated at the rate of return acceptable to the management (Cost of capital is generally taken)
- Working capital is taken as a cash outflow in the year the project starts commercial production.

Formula to calculate the NPV:

$$NPV = [\frac{R_1}{(1+k)^1} + \frac{R_2}{(1+k)^2} + \cdots + \frac{R_n}{(1+k)^n}] - 1$$

Where,

NPV = Net present value

R= Cash Inflows at different periods

K = Cost of capital (or) cut-off rate

I = Cash outflows at different periods

Accept / Reject Criterion

NPV > Zero (or) If NPV is positive accept the project

NPV < Zero (or) If NPV is negative reject the project

NPV = 0 Indifferent (or) Indeterminate

Advantages

- It takes into account the entire economic life of the project's investment and income.
- It considers the time value of money and the interest rate.
- This can be applied with uniform cash flows and uneven cash flows or cash flows at different periods of time.
- It is consistent with the objective of maximizing the welfare of owners.
- It tries to maximize the profit.
- It favoring more profitable projects.

Disadvantages

- It is difficult to understand and complicated to operate.
- It is not easy to determine an appropriate discount rate.
- It is very difficult to forecast the exact economic life of an investment.
- It may not give satisfactory result when the project involves different amounts of investment.
- Shorter span of life of the assets.

Calculation of NPV in case of replacement of machine

- Additional investment
- Net operating savings or profit
- Additional tax

Present Value Index Method or Profitability Index Method

The profitability index is also known as Benefit cost ratio. It shows the relationship between P.V. of cash inflows and P.V of cash inflows.

$$P.I. = \frac{\text{Present value of future cash inflows}}{\text{Present value of future cash outflows}}$$

Accept / Reject criterion:

PI > 1 accept the project

PI < 1 reject the project

In case of more than one project, project with higher present value index will be accepted.

Advantages

- Profitability index method is most suitable to evaluate the project.

Disadvantages

- This method is difficult to understand and work out as compared to other methods of ranking capital investment proposals.

Internal Rate of Return Method

Under this method a discount rate or a rate of return is calculated. This rate is called internal rate of return which is the maximum rate of interest that could be paid for the capital employed over the economic life of an investment without any loss on the project.

Internal rate of return is that rate at which the sum of discounted cash inflows equals the sum of discounted cash outflows.

$$IRR = \frac{\text{Cash inflows}}{\text{Cash outflows}}$$

If return is for only one year:

$$I = \frac{R}{I + r}$$

If return is over a number of years:

$$I = [\frac{R_1}{(1+r)^1} + \frac{R_2}{(1+r)^2} + \cdots + \frac{R_n}{(1+r)^n}]$$

Where,

I = Cash outflows at different periods

R = Cash inflows at different periods

R = Rate of return on the investment

IRR is also known as trial and error yield method.

If the cash inflows are uneven the IRR can be calculated as follows:

$$F = \frac{I}{C}$$

Where,

F = Factor to be located

I = Initial investment

C = Average annual cash inflow

Accept / Reject Criterion

- Single project – A project is accepted if IRR exceeds the cut-off rate.
- Two or More projects – A project giving a higher internal rate of return would be preferred.

Advantages

- It takes into time value of money.
- True profitability of a project can be assessed.
- It considers the profitability of a project over its entire economic life
- Cost of capital or pre-determined Cut-off rate is not required.
- It is better than NPV and IP method.
- Ranking of various proposals.
- It provides for maximizing profitability
- It is considered to be a more flexible technique of capital budgeting.

Disadvantages

- In IRR the discounting rate is the unknown factor.
- IRR determine the maximum interest.
- IRR assumes re-investment.
- It is more practical.
- It may differ from project evaluation
- It is difficult to understand.

Net Present Value Method Vs Internal Rate of Return Method

Similarities

- All profitable independent investment proposals can be accepted or rejected without constraints on the basis of a minimum required rate of return.
- Conventional investment proposal which involves cash outflows or outlays in the initial period followed by a series of cash inflows.
- In case of the NPV Method, a proposal is accepted if its NPV is positive i.e., when actual rate or return on investment is higher than the cut-off rate. In IRR method, a proposal is accepted only when the IRR is higher than the cut-off rate.

Differences

S. No.	NPV	IRR
1.	Interest rate is known.	Interest rate is to be calculated.
2.	The present value is determined by discounting the future cash flows of a project at a specified rate called the cut off rate based on cost of capital.	But under this method cash flows are discounted at a suitable rate which equates present value of the cash inflows and outflows.
3.	Recongnises the importance of market rate of interest or cost of capital.	Does not consider the market rate of interest.
4.	Intermediate cash flows are presumed to be reinvested at the cut-off rate	Intermediate cash flows are presumed to be reinvested at the internal rate of return.

2.2. Cost of Capital

2.2.1. Introduction

The cost of capital of a firm is the minimum rate of return expected by its investors. It is the weighted average cost of various sources of finance used by the firm. The capital used by the firm may be in the form of debt, preference capital, retained earnings and equity shares. The concept of cost of capital is very important in the financial management. Cost of capital for a firm may be defined as the cost of obtaining funds i.e., the average rate of return that the investors in a firm would expect for supplying funds to the firm.

According to Solomin Ezra: "Cost of capital is the minimum required rate of earning or the cutoff rate of capital expenditure."

According to Jhon J: "The rate of return the firm requires from investment in order to increase the value of the firm in then market place."

Features of Cost of Capital

1. Cost of capital is not a cost as such. In fact, it is the rate of return that a firm requires earning from its projects.
2. It is the minimum rate of return. Cost of Capital of a firm is that minimum rate of return, which will at least maintain the market value of the firm.
3. It comprises of three elements.

$$K = r + b + f + o$$

Where,

K= cost of capital

r = The expected normal rate of return at zero risk level

b= premium for business risk

f = premium for finance risk

o =other risk

Cost of Capital

1. RISK FREE
2. FINANCIAL RISK
3. BUSINESS RISK

2.2.2. *Significance of Cost of Capital*

1. As Acceptance Criteria in Capital Budgeting: The concept of cost of capital has assumed growing importance largely because of the needs to devise a rational mechanism for making the investment decision of the firm. Considering the fusion capital can make capital budgeting decisions. According to the present value method of capital budgeting, if the present value of expected returns from investment is greater than or equal to the cost of investment, the project may be accepted, otherwise it may be rejected.
2. As a Determinant of Capital Mix in Capital Structure Decisions: Financing the firm asset is the very crucial problem in every business and as a general rule there should

be a proper mix of debt and equity capital in financing the firm's assets. While designing the optimal capital structure, the management g\has to keep in mind the on\objective of maximizing the value of the firm and minimizing the cost of capital.

3. As a Basis for Evaluating the Financial Performance: The concept of cost of capital can be used to evaluate the financial performance of the top management. The actual profitability of the project is compared the projected overall cost of capital and the actual cost of capital of funds rise to finance the project if the actual profitability of the project is more than the projected.

As the Basis for taking other Financial decisions: The cost of capital is also used in making other financial decisions such as dividend policy, capitalization of profits, making the right issue and working capital.

2.2.3. Computation of Cost of Capital

Computation of overall cost of capital of a firm involves: Computation of cost of Specific source of finance

1. Cost of Debt
2. Cost of Preference Capital
3. Cost of Equity Capital
4. Cost of Retained earnings
5. Weighted average cost of capital

Computation of cost of Specific source of finance

Cost of Debt: The cost of debt is the rate of interest payable on debt.

Cost of perpetual / Irredeemable Debt

Before tax cost of debt

$$Kdb = \frac{I}{P}$$

Where, Kdb = before tax cost of debt

I = Interest

P = Principal

In case if debt is raised at premium or discount, P would be considered as the amount of net proceeds received from the issue and not the face value of the securities. The formula may changed to

$$Kdb = \frac{I}{NP}$$

Where NP = Net proceeds

After Tax Cost of Debt

$$\mathbf{Kda = Kdb\ (1\text{-}t)}$$

Where, Kda = after tax cost of debt

t = Rate of tax

Cost of Redeemable Debt: Usually the debt is issued to be redeemed after a certain period during the lifetime of the firm. Such a debt issue is known as Redeemable Debt. The cost of Redeemable debt may be computed as:

Before Tax Cost of Debt

$$Kdb = \frac{I + \frac{1}{N}(RV\text{-}NP)}{\frac{1}{2}(RVP + NP)}$$

Where, I = Interest

N = Number of years in which debt is to be redeemed

RV = Redeemable value of debt

NP = Net Proceeds

After Tax cost of debt, Kda = Kdb (1-t)

Cost of Equity Share Capital

The cost of the equity is the "maximum rate of return that the company must earn on equity financed portion of its investments in order to leave unchanged the market price of its stock." The cost of equity capital is a function of the expected return by its investors.

The cost of equity can be computed in the following ways:

Dividend Yield method or Dividend / Price Ratio method: According to this method the cost of equity capital is the discount rate that equates the present value of expected future dividend per share with the net proceeds of a share.

$$Ke = \frac{D}{NP}$$

OR

$$Ke = \frac{D}{NP}$$

Where, Ke = Cost of Equity Capital

D = Expected Dividend per share

NP = Net Proceeds per share

MP = Market Price per share

2.2.4. Computation of Weighted Average Cost of Capital

Weighted average cost of capital is the average cost of various sources of financing. It is also known as Composite Cost of Capital, Overall Cost of capital, average accost of capital. Once the cost of specific source of capital is determined, weighted average cost of capital can be computed by putting weights to the specific costs of capital in proportion of the various sources of funds to the total. The CIMA defines the weighted average cost of capital " as the average cost of company's finance (equity, debentures, bank loans) weighted according to the proportion each elements bears to the total pool of capital, weighting is usually based on market valuation current yields and costs after tax."

CHAPTER 3

FINANCING AND DIVIDEND DECISION

3.1. Financing and Operating Leverage

3.1.1. Definition

Leverage is the employment of assets or funds for which the firm pays a fixed cost or fixed return.

The leverage formally termed as 'fixed financial cost'. It should be noted that fixed cost or return is the fulcrum of leverage. If a firm is not required to pay fixed cost of fixed return, there will be no leverage.

3.1.2. Types of Leverage

- Operating leverage
- Financial leverage
- Combined/Composite leverage

3.1.2.1 Operating Leverage

The leverage associated with investment activities is referred to as operating leverage. Operating leverage is determined by the relationship between the firm's sales revenues and its earnings before interest and taxes (EBIT). The earnings before interest and taxes are also generally called operating profit.

Definition

The operating leverage may be defined as a tendency of the operating profit to vary disproportionately with sales. It is said to exist when the firm has to pay fixed cost regardless of volume of output/sales.

The firm is said to have a high degree of operating leverage if it employs a greater amount of fixed cost and small amount of variable cost. On the other hand, a firm has low operating leverage when it employs a greater amount of variable costs and smaller amount of fixed cost.

Operating leverage results from the existence of operating expenses. The operating cost fall into three categories.

- Fixed cost
- Variable cost

- Semi-variable cost

$$\text{Operating leverage} = \frac{\text{Contribution}}{\text{Operating profit}} \text{ or } \frac{C}{OP}$$

Here, operating profit = EBIT

Operating leverage may be

- Favourable
    - The contribution exceeds the fixed costs.
- Unfavourable
    - Fixed cost exceeds the contribution.

3.1.2.2 Financial Leverage

Financial leverage refers to leverage associated with the financing is called financial leverage. It represents the relationship between the firm's earnings before interest and taxes and the earnings available for ordinary shareholders.

Financial leverage results from the presence of fixed finance changes in the firm's income steam. These fixed charges do not vary with the EBIT or operating profits.

Definition

The financial leverage may be defined as, "*tendency of the residual net income to vary disproportionately with operating profit. It indicates the change that takes place in the taxable income as a result of fixed dividend bearing securities in the total capital structure of the company*".

- Favourable financial leverage or positive financial leverage
- Unfavourable financial leverage or Negative financial leverage

1. ***Favourable Financial Leverage***

When the firm earns more on the assets purchased with the funds, than the fixed cost of their use.

2. ***Unfavourable Financial Leverage***

When the firm does not earns as much as the funds cost.

The effect of earning by the use of long-term fixed cost securities, such as preference shares and debentures, is called financial leverage.

$$\text{Financial leverage} = \frac{\text{Operating profit}}{\text{Profit Before tax}} \text{ or } \frac{OP}{PBT} \text{ or } \frac{EBIT}{PBT}$$

Where,

EBIT = Earnings Before Interest and Tax

OP = Operating Profit

PBT = Profit Before Tax

Trading on Equity and Financial Leverage

The use of long-term fixed interest bearing debt and preference share capital along with equity share capital is called trading on equity.

Financial leverage is also known as 'trading on equity'. However, most of authors of financial management are of the option that the term trading on equity should be used for the term financial leverage only when the financial leverage is favourable.

3.1.2.3Combined/Composite Leverage

This leverage shows the relationship between a change in sales and the corresponding variation in taxable income.

$$\text{Combined leverage} = \frac{\text{Contribution}}{\text{PBT}} \text{ or O. L x F. L}$$

3.1.3. Degree of Operating Leverage

Operating leverage can be defined in terms of degree of operating leverage. The degree of operating leverage measured in quantitative terms the extent or degree of operating leverage. When proportionate change is EBIT as a result of a given changes in sales is more than the proportionate change in sales.

Definition

The DOL of operating leverage may be defined as, "percentage change in the profit resulting from a percentage change in the sales".

Formula

$$\text{Degree of Operating leverage} = \frac{\text{Percentage changes in EBIT}}{\text{Percentage changes in Sales}}$$

Or

$$\text{Degree of Operating leverage} = \frac{\text{Contribution}}{\text{EBIT}}$$

Utility

- The operating leverage indicates the impact of change in sales on operating income.
- If a firm has a high degree of operating leverage, a small change in sales will have a large effect on operating income.
- EBIT of such a firm will increase at a faster than the increase in sales.
- EBIT of such a firm will suffer a greater loss as compared to reduction in its sales.
- The firm does not like to operate under conditions of high degree of operating leverage.

DOL > 1 implies there is opening leverage exist

DOL = 1 implies there is no operating leverage; it happen then there is no fixed cost.

Operating Leverage vs Financial Leverage

S. No.	Operating leverage	Financial leverage
1.	Related to the investment activities.	More concerned with financial matters.
2.	It is useful to take capital expenditure decision.	It is useful for mixing the debt and equity in the capital structure.
3.	The fluctuation in the EBIT can be predicted.	The changes of EPS due to the debt-equity mix are predicted.
4.	It is used to predict business risk.	It is used to predict the financial risk.

Significance of Leverage

- It is useful to measure the return to the owners and the market price of the equity shares.
- Financial and operating leverages are important tools to plan a balanced capital structure and maximize the return on shares.
- A firm with a low operating leverage will gain by having a high financial leverage, if it has enough profitable opportunities for the employment of borrowed funds.
- Financial leverage is an important tool in the hands of financial management. If used carefully, it can maximize the return to shareholders. A firm with low operating leverage and high financial leverage is considered an ideal situation for the maximization of profits with minimum risk.

Limitations of Financial Leverage

- It can be used to increase the EPS only when the rate of earnings of the company is more than the fixed rate of interest. On the other hand, if it does not earn as much as the cost of interest bearing securities, then it will work adversely and hence cannot be employed.
- It is beneficial only to the companies having stable and regular earnings.

3.1.4. *Earning Per Share (EPS)*

Earning per share (EPS) is the amount that the shareholder can get on every share hold. It is calculated from the following.

$$\text{EPS} = \frac{\text{Net profit available to equity shareholders}}{\text{Number of ordinary shares outstanding}}$$

Degree of Financial Leverage

The degree of financial leverage measures the impact of a change is operating income on change in earnings on equity capital. It can be calculated as:

$$\text{Degree of financial leverage (DFL)} = \frac{\text{Percentage change in EPS}}{\text{Percentage change in EBIT}} \text{ or } \frac{\text{EBIT}}{\text{PBT}}$$

Degree of Operating Leverage

The degree of operating leverage is the percentage change in the profits resulting from a percentage change in the sales. It can be calculated as:

$$\text{Degree of operating leverage} = \frac{\text{Percentage change in profits}}{\text{Percentage change in sales}}$$

3.2. Capital Structure

In order to run and manage the company, funds are needed. Right from the promotional stage up to end, finances play an important role in the company's life. If funds are inadequate, the business suffers and if the funds are not properly managed. The entire organization suffers. It is therefore; necessary that correct estimate of the current and future needs of the capital to be made to have an optimum capital structure.

The capital structure is made up of debt and equity securities and refers to permanent financing of a firm. It is composed of long-term debt, preference share capital and shareholder's funds.

According to Gestenberg: "Capital structure of a company refers to the composition or make up of its capitalization and it includes all long-term capital resources viz: loans, reserves, shares and bonds". Forms of capital structure

- Equity shares only
- Equity and preference Shares
- Equity Shares and Debentures
- Equity, preference and Debentures.

3.2.1. *Theories of Capital Structure*

Different kinds of theories have been propounded by different authors to explain the relationship between Capital structure and cost of capital and value of the firm. The important theories are:

1. Net income approach
2. Net Operating Income approach
3. The Traditional approach
4. Modigliani and Miller approach

Assumptions: In discussing the theories of capital structure, the following assumptions have been used:

1. There are only two sources of finance i.e. equity and debt
2. There would be no change in the investment decision.
3. That the firm has a policy of distributing the entire profits among the shareholders implying that there is no retained earnings.
4. The operating profits of the firm are given and nor expected to grow.
5. The business risk complexion of the firm is given and is not affected by the financing mix.
6. There is no corporate and personal tax.

In discussing the theories of capital structure, the following definitions and notations have been used:

E = Total market value of the Equity

D = Total market value of the Debt

V = Total market value of the firm i.e., D + E

I = Total Interest Payment

NOP = Net operating profit i.e. EBIT

NP = Net Profit or profit after Tax

Do = Dividend paid by the company at Time o

D1 = Expected Dividend at the end of the year 1

Po = Current market price of the Share

P1 = Expected Market Price of the share after 1 year.

Kd = After Tax Cost of Debt i.e. I/D

Ke = Cost of Equity i.e. D/Po

Ko = Overall Cost of Capital i.e. WACC

1. Net Income Approach: According to Durand, this theory states that there is a relationship between Capital structure and the value of the Firm and therefore the firm Can affects its value by increasing or decreasing the Debt proportion in the overall financing mix. This approach is based on the following assumptions.
   1. The total Capital requirement of the firm is given and remains constant.
   2. The cost of debt is less than cost of Equity.
   3. Both Kd and Ke remain constant and increase in financial leverage i.e. use of more and debt financing in the capital structure does not affect the risk perception of the investors. The line of argument in favor of Net Income approach is that as the proportion of Debt financing in capital structure increases, the proportion of an expensive source of fund increases. This results in the decrease in overall cost of capital leading to an increase in the value of the firm. The reason for assuming Kd less than Ke are that interest rates are usually lower than the dividend rates due to the element of risk and the benefit of tax as the interest is a deductible expense. The total market value of the firm on the basis of Net Income approach can be ascertained as below:

V = E + D

Where V = Total market value of the firm

E = Total market value of the Equity

$$= \frac{Earnings\ available\ to\ equity\ shareholder\ (NP)}{Equity\ Capitalization\ rate\ (Ke)}$$

D = Total market value of the Debt.

Overall cost of Capital can be calculated as below:

$$Ko = \frac{EBIT}{V}$$

2. Net Operating Income Approach: The NOI approach is opposite to the NI approach. According to NOI approach, the market value of the firm depends upon the net operating profit or EBIT and the overall cost of Capital. The financing mix or the capital structure is irrelevant and does not affect the value of the firm. The NOI approach makes the following assumptions:
   1. The Kd is taken as constant.
   2. The K0 of the firm is also taken as constant.
   3. The firm capitalizes the total earnings of the firm to find the value of the firm as a whole.

4. The use of more and more debt in capital structure increase the risk of the shareholders and thus results in the increase in cost of equity capital i.e. Ke. The increase in Ke is such as to completely offset the benefits of employing cheaper debts.

The value of a firm on the basis of NOI approach can be determined as below:

$$V = \frac{EBIT}{Ko}$$

Where, V = Value of the firm

EBIT = Earning before interest and tax

Ko = Overall cost of Capital

The market value of equity is residual value, calculated as

$$E = V - D$$

And the Cost of Equity is, $Ke = \frac{EBIT - Interest}{V-D}$

Thus financing Mix is irrelevant and does not affects the value of the firm.. The value of the firm remains for all types of debt–equity mix. Since there will be change in the risk of the shareholders as a result of change in Debt-Equity mix, therefore the Ke will be changing linearly with change in debt proportion.

3. Traditional Approach: The traditional approach also known as Intermediate approach is a compromise between the two extremes of Net income approach and Net operating income approach. According to this theory, the value of the firm can be increased initially or the cost of capital can be decreased by using more debt as the debt is the cheaper source if finance then equity. Thus the optimum capital structure can be reached by a proper Debt Equity mix. Beyond a particular point, the cost of equity increases because increased debt increases the financial risk of the equity shareholders. The advantage of cheaper debt at this point of capital structure is offset by increased cost of equity. After this there comes a stage, when the increased cost of equity cannot be offset by the advantage of low cost debt. Thus the overall cost of debt decrease up to a certain point, remains more or less unchanged for l\moderate increase in debt thereafter and increases or rises beyond a certain point. Thus as per the traditional approach, a firm can be benefited from a moderate level of leverage when then advantages of using debt outweighed the disadvantages of increasing Ke. The overall cost of capital is a function of financial leverage. The value of the firm can be affected, by the judicious use of debt and equity in capital structure.

4. Modigliani and Miller Approach: M&M Model, which was presented in 1958 on the relationship between the leverage, cost of capital and the value of the firm. The model emphasis that under a given set of assumptions the capital structure and its composition has no effect on the value of the firm. There is nothing which may be called the optimal capital structure, the model is based ob the following assumptions:
   1. The capital markets are perfect and the complete information is available to all the investors free of cost.
   2. The securities are infinitely divisible.
   3. Investors are rational and well informed about the risk return of all the securities.
   4. The personal leverage and the corporate leverage are perfect substitute.

   On the basis of the above assumptions, the M&M Model derived that:

   1. The total value of the firm is equal to the capitalized value of the operating earnings of the firm.
   2. The total value of the firm is independent of the financial mix.
   3. The cut off rate of the investment decision of the firm depends upon the risk class to which the firm belongs, and thus is not affected by the financing pattern of this investment.
   4. The M&M model argues that if two firms are alike in all respects except that they differ in respect of their financing patter and their market value, then the investors will develop a tendency to sell the shares of the overvalued firm and to buy the shares of the undervalued firm.

3.3. Dividend Decision

The term dividend refers to that part of profits of a company which is distributed by the company among its shareholders. It is the reward of the shareholders for investments made by them in the shares of the company. The investors are interested in earning the maximum return on their investments and to maximize their wealth. A company, on the other hand, needs to provide funds to finance its long-term growth. If a company pays out as dividend most of what it earns, then for business requirements and further expansion it will have to depend upon outside resources such as issue of debt or new shares. Dividend policy of a firm, thus affects both the long-term financing and the wealth of shareholders.

Dividend Decision and Value of Firms: The value of the firm can be maximized if the shareholders' wealth is maximized. There are conflicting views regarding the impact of dividend decision on the valuation of the firm. According to one school of thought, dividend decision does not affect the share-holders' wealth and hence the valuation of the firm. On the other hand, according to the other school of thought, dividend decision materially affects the shareholders' wealth and also the valuation of the firm. We will discuss below the views of the two schools of thought under two groups:

1. The Irrelevance Concept of Dividend or the Theory of Irrelevance, and
2. The Relevance Concept of Dividend or the Theory of Relevance.

The Irrelevance Concept of Dividend or the Theory of Irrelevance:

Residual Approach: According to this theory, dividend decision has no effect on the wealth of the shareholders or the prices of the shares, and hence it is irrelevant so far as the valuation of the firm is concerned. This theory regards dividend decision merely as a part of financing decision because the earnings available may be retained in the business for re-investment. But, if the funds are not required in the business they may be distributed as dividends. This theory assumes that investors do not differentiate between dividends and retentions by the firm. Their basic desire is to earn higher return on their investment. In case the firm has profitable investment opportunities giving a higher rate of return than the cost of retained earnings, the investors would be content with the firm retaining the earnings to finance the same. However, if the firm is not in a position to find profitable investment opportunities, the investors would prefer to receive the earnings in the form of dividends. Thus, a firm should retain the earnings if it has profitable investment opportunities otherwise it should pay them as dividends.

Modlgliani and Miller Approach (MM Model): Modigliani and Miller have expressed in the most comprehensive manner in support of the theory of irrelevance. They maintain that dividend policy has no effect on the market price of the shares and the value of the firm is determined by the earning capacity of the firm or its investment policy. The splitting of earnings between retentions and dividends, may be in any manner the firm likes, does not affect the value of the firm. As observed by M.M. "Under conditions of perfect capital markets, rational investors, absence of tax discrimination between dividend income and capital appreciation, given the firm's investment policy, its dividend policy may have no influence on the market price of the shares.'"

Assumptions of MM Hypothesis

a. There are perfect capital markets.
b. Investors behave rationally.
c. Information about the company is available to all without any cost.
d. There are no floatation and transaction costs.

e. No investor is large enough to affect the market price of shares.

f. There are no taxes or there are no differences in the tax rates applicable to dividends and capital gains.

g. The firm has a rigid investment policy.

The Argument of MM: The argument given by MM in support of their hypothesis is that whatever increase in the value of the firm results from the payment of dividend, will be exactly off set by the decline in the market price of shares because of external financing and there will be no change in the total wealth of the shareholders. For example, if a company, having investment opportunities, distributes all its earnings among the shareholders, it will have to raise additional funds from external sources. This will result in the increase in number of shares or payment of interest charges, resulting in fall in the earnings per share in the future. Thus whatever a shareholder gains on account of dividend payment is neutralized completely by the fall in the market price of shares due to decline in expected future earnings per share. To be more specific, the market price of a share in the beginning of a period is equal to the present value of dividends paid at the end of the period plus the market price of the shares at the end of the period.

This can be put in the form of the following formula:

$$P0 = \frac{D1 + P1}{1 + Ke}$$

Where, P0 = Market price per share at the beginning of the period, or prevailing market price of a share.

D1 = Dividend to be received at the end of the period.

P 1 = Market price per share at the end of the period.

Ke = Cost of equity capital or rate of capitalization.

Criticism of MM Approach

1. Prefect capital market does not exist in reality
2. Information about the company is not available to .all the persons.
3. The firms have to incur flotation costs while issuing 'securities.
4. Taxes do exit and there is normally different tax treatment for dividends and capital gains.
5. The firms do not follow a rigid investment policy.
6. The investors have to pay brokerage, fees, etc. while doing any transaction.
7. Shareholders may prefer current income as compared to further gains.

The Relevance Concept of Dividend or The Theory of Relevance: The other school of thought on dividend decision holds that the dividend decisions considerably affect the value of the firm. The advocates of this school of thought include Myron Gordon, James Walter and Richardson. According to them dividends communicate information to the investors about the firms' profitability and hence dividend decision becomes relevant. Those firms which pay higher dividends, will have greater value as compared to those which do not pay dividends or have a lower dividend payout ratio.

We have examined below two theories representing this notion:

(i) Walter's Approach, and (ii) Gordon's Approach

Walter's Approach: Prof. Walter's approach supports the doctrine that dividend decisions are relevant and affect the value of the firm. Prof. Walter's model is based on the relationship between the firm's (i) return on investment. i.e. r. and (ii) the cost of capital or the required rate of return, i.e., k.·

According to Prof. Walter, If $r > k$ i.e., if the firm earns a higher rate of return on its investment than the required rate of return, the firm should retain the earnings. Such 'firms are termed as growth firm and the optimum pay-out would be zero in their case.

In case of declining firms which do not have profitable investments, i.e., where $r < k$, the shareholders would stand to gain if the firm distributes its earnings. For such firms, the optimum pay-out would be 100% and the firms should distribute the entire earnings as dividends.

In case of normal firms where $r = k$, the dividend policy will not affect the market value of shares as the shareholders will get the same return from the firm as expected by them. For such firms, there is no optimum dividend payout and the value of the firm would not change with the change in dividend rate.

Assumption of Walter's Model

a. The investments of the firm are financed through retained earnings only and the firm does not use external sources of funds.
b. The internal rate of return (r) and the cost of capital (k) of the firm are constant.
c. Earnings and dividends do not change while determining the value.
d. The firm has a very long life.

Criticism of Walter's Model

The basic assumption that investments are financed through retained earnings only is seldom true in real world. Firms do raise funds by external financing. The internal rate of return, i.e. r, also does not, remain constant. As a matter of fact, with increased investment the rate of return also changes. The assumption that cost of capital (k) will remain constant also does not hold good. As a firm's risk pattern does not remain constant, it is not proper to assume that k will always remain constant.

Gordon's Approach: Myron Gordon has also developed a model on the lines of Prof. Walter suggesting that dividends are relevant and the dividend decision of the firm affects its value. His basic valuation model is based on the following assumptions:

a. The firm is an all equity firm.
b. No external financing is available or used. Retained earnings are the only Source of finance.
c. The rate of return on the firm's investment r, is constant.
d. The retention ratio, b, is constant. Thus, the growth rate of the firm $g = br$, is also constant.
e. The cost of capital for the firm remains constant and it is greater than the growth rate, i.e. $k > br$.
f. The firm has perpetual life.
g. Corporate taxes do not exist.

3.3.1. Determinants of Dividend Policy

The payment of dividend involves some legal as well as financial considerations. The following are the important factors which determine the dividend policy of a firm:

1. Legal Restrictions: Legal provisions relating to dividends in the Companies Act, 1956 lay down a framework within which dividend policy is formulated. These provisions require that:
    - Dividend can be paid only out of current profits or past profits after providing for depreciation or out of the moneys provided by Government for the payment of dividends in pursuance of a guarantee given by the Government.
    - A company providing more than ten per cent dividend is required to transfer certain percentage of the current year's profits to reserves.
    - The dividends cannot be paid out of capital, because it will amount to reduction of capital adversely affecting the security of its creditors.

2. Magnitude and Trend of Earnings: As dividends can be paid only out of present or past year's profits, earnings of a company fix the upper limits on dividends. The dividends should, generally, be paid out of current year's earnings only as the retained earnings of the previous years become more or less a part of permanent investment in the business to earn current profits. The past trend of the company's earnings should also be kept in consideration while making the dividend decision.
3. Desire and Type of Shareholders: Desires of shareholders for dividends depend upon their economic status. Investors, such as retired persons, widows and other economically weaker persons view dividends as a source of funds to meet their day-to-day living expenses. To benefit such investors, the companies should pay regular dividends. On the other hand, a wealthy investor in a high income tax bracket may not benefit by high current dividend incomes. Such an investor may be interested in lower current dividends and high capital gains.
4. Nature of Industry: Certain industries have a comparatively steady and stable demand irrespective of the prevailing economic conditions. For instance, people used to drink liquor both in boom as well as in recession. Such firms expect regular earnings and hence can follow a consistent dividend policy. On the other hand. If the earnings are uncertain, as in the case of luxury goods, conservative policy should be followed.
5. Age of the Company: The age of the company also influences the dividend decision of a company. A newly established concern has to limit payment of dividend and retain substantial part of earnings for financing its future growth and development, while older companies which have established sufficient reserves can afford to pay liberal dividends.
6. Future Financial Requirements: The management of a concern has to reconcile the conflicting interests of shareholders and those of the company's financial needs. If a company has highly profitable investment opportunities it can convince the shareholders of the need for limitation of dividend to increase the future earnings.
7. Economic Policy: The dividend policy of a firm has also to be adjusted to the economic policy of the Government as was the case when the Temporary Restriction on Payment of Dividend Ordinance was in force. In 1974 and 1975, companies were allowed to pay dividends not more than 33 per cent of their profits or 12 per cent on the paid-up value of the shares, whichever was lower.
8. Taxation Policy: The taxation policy of the Government also affects the dividend decision of a firm. A high or low rate of business taxation affects the net earnings of company (after tax) and thereby its dividend policy. Similarly, a firm's dividend policy may be dictated by

the income-tax status of its shareholders. If the dividend income of shareholders is heavily taxed being in high income bracket, the shareholders may forego cash dividend and prefer bonus shares and capital gains.

9. Inflation: Inflation acts as a constraint in the payment of dividends. when prices .rise, funds generated by depreciation would not be adequate to replace fixed assets, and hence to maintain the same assets and capital intact, substantial part of the current earnings would be retained. Otherwise, imaginary and inflated book profits in the days of rising prices would amount to payment of dividends much more than warranted by the real profits, out of the equity capital resulting in erosion of capital.
10. Control Objectives: As in case of a high dividend pay-out ratio, the retained earnings are insignificant and the company will have to issue new shares to raise funds to finance its future requirements. The control of the existing shareholders will be diluted if they cannot buy the additional shares issued by the company.
11. Requirements of Institutional Investors: Dividend policy of a company can be affected by the requirements of institutional investors such as financial institutions, banks insurance corporations, etc. These investors usually favor a policy of regular payment of cash dividends and stipulate their own terms with regard to payment of dividend on equity shares.
12. Stability of Dividends: Stability of dividend simply refers to the payment of dividend regularly and shareholders, generally, prefer payment of such regular dividends. Some companies follow a policy of constant dividend per share while others follow a policy of constant payout ratio and while there are some other who follows a policy of constant low dividend per share plus an extra dividend in the years of high profits.
13. Liquid Resources: The dividend policy of a firm is also influenced by the availability of liquid resources. Although, a firm may have sufficient available profits to declare dividends, yet it may not be desirable to pay dividends if it does not have sufficient liquid resources. If a company does not have liquid resources, it is better to declare stock dividend i.e. issue of bonus shares to the existing shareholders. The issue of bonus shares also amounts to distribution of firm's earnings among the existing shareholders without affecting its cash position.

Types of Dividend Policy

The various types of dividend policies are discussed as follows:

1. Regular Dividend Policy: Payment of dividend at the usual rate is termed as regular dividend. The investors such as retired persons, widows and other economically

weaker persons prefer to get regular dividends. Advantages of regular dividend policy: (i) It establishes a profitable record of the company. (ii) It creates confidence amongst the shareholders. (iii) It aids in long-term financing and renders financing easier. (iv) It stabilizes the market value of shares. (v) The ordinary shareholders view dividends as a source of funds to meet their day-to-day living expenses. (vi) If profits are not distributed regularly and are retained, the shareholders may have to pay a higher rate of tax in the year when accumulated profits are distributed. However, it must be remembered that regular dividends can be maintained only by companies of long standing and stable earnings.

2. Stable Dividend Policy: The term 'stability of dividends' means consistency in the stream of dividend payments. In more precise terms, it means payment of certain minimum amount of dividend regularly. A stable dividend policy may be established in any of the following three forms: (i) Constant dividend per share. Policy of paying fixed dividend per share irrespective of the level of earnings year after year. Such firms, usually, create a 'Reserve for Dividend Equalization' to enable them pay the fixed dividend even in the year when the earnings are not sufficient. (ii) Constant payout ratio. Constant pay-out ratio means payment of a fixed percentage of net earnings as dividends every year. The amount of dividend in such a policy fluctuates in direct proportion to the earnings of the company. (iii) Stable rupee dividend plus extra dividend. Some' companies follow a policy of paying constant low dividend per share plus an extra dividend in the years of high profits. Such a policy is most suitable to the firm having fluctuating earnings from year to year. Advantages of Stable Dividend Policy: (i) It is sign of continued normal operations of the company. (ii) It stabilizes the market value of shares (iii) It creates confidence among the investors, improves credit standing and makes financing easier (iv) It provides a source of livelihood to those investors who view dividends as a source of fund to meet day-to-day expenses (v) It meets the requirements of institutional investors who prefer companies with stable divide.
3. Irregular Dividend Policy: Some companies follow irregular dividend payments on account of the following: (i) Uncertainty of earnings(ii) Unsuccessful business operations(iii) Lack of liquid resources
4. No Dividend Policy: A company can follow a policy of paying no dividends presently because of its unfavorable working capital position or on account of requirements of funds for future expansion and growth.

3.3.2. *Forms of Dividend*

Dividends can be classified in various forms. Dividends paid in the ordinary course of bus in known as Profit dividends, while dividends paid out of capital are known as Liquidation dividends. A dividend which is declared between two annual general meetings is called interim dividend, while the dividend recommended to the shareholders at the annual general meeting is known as final dividend.

Classification on the Basis of Medium in which they are Paid

a. Cash Dividend: A cash dividend is a usual method of paying dividends. Payment of cash results in outflow of funds and reduces the company's net worth, though the shareholders get a opportunity to invest the cash in any manner they desire. This is why the ordinary shareholders prefer to dividends in cash.
b. Scrip or Bond Dividend: A scrip dividend promises to pay the shareholders at a future specific date. In case a company does not have sufficient funds to pay dividends in cash, it may issue notes or bonds for amount due to the shareholders. The objective of scrip dividend is to postpone the immediate Payment. A scrip dividend bears interest and is accepted as a collateral security.
c. Property Dividend: Property dividends are paid in the form of some assets other than cash are distributed under exceptional circumstances and are not popular in India.
d. Stock Dividend: Stock dividend means the issue of bonus shares to the existing shareholders. If a company does not have liquid resources it is better to declare stock dividend. Stock dividend amounts to capitalization of earnings and distribution of profits among the existing shareholders without affecting the cash position of the firm. This has been discussed in detail under "Bonus Issue".

Bonus Issue

A company can pay bonus to its shareholders either in cash or in the form of shares. Many a times, a company is not in a position to pay bonus in cash in spite of sufficient profits because of unsatisfactory cash position or because of its adverse effects on the working capital of the company. In such cases, if the articles of association of the company provide, it can pay bonus to its shareholder in the form of shares by making partly paid shares as fully paid or by the issue of fully paid bonus shares. Issue of bonus shares in lieu of dividend is not allowed as according to Section 205 of the Companies Act, 1956, no dividend can be paid except in cash. It cannot be termed as a gift because it only represents the past sacrifice of the shareholders. When a company accumulates huge profits and reserves, its balance sheet does not reveal a true picture about the capital structure of the company and the shareholders do not get fair return on their capital. Thus, if the Articles of Association of the company so permit, the excess amount can be distributed among the existing shareholders of the company by way of issue of bonus shares.

The effect of bonus issue is two-fold:

a. It amounts to reduction in the amount of accumulated profits and reserves.
b. There is a corresponding increase in the paid up share capital of the company.

CHAPTER 4

WORKING CAPITAL MANAGEMENT

4.1. Principles of Working Capital

4.1.1. Introduction

Meaning of Working Capital: Capital required for the business can be of two types:

1. Fixed Capital
2. Working Capital

Fixed capital is required to create the production facilities through purchase of fixed assets like Land, Machinery, and Building etc. Investment in these assets represents that part of firm's capital, which is blocked on permanent or fixed basis and is called fixed capital. Funds are also needed for short-term purpose for the purchase of Raw material, Payment of Wages etc. these funds are known as Working Capital. In simple words, working capital refers to that part of firm's capital, which is required for financing short-term assets.

Definitions of Working Capital: According to Shubin: "Working Capital is the amount of funds necessary to cover the cost of operating the enterprises." According to Genestenberg: "

Working Capital means current assets of a comp-any that are changed in the ordinary course of business from one form to another as for e.g. Cash to inventories, inventories to receivables and receivables to cash".

4.1.2. Concept of Working Capital

Working capital means excess of current assets over current liabilities. Funds invested in current assets are known as "Gross working capital". The difference between current assets and current liabilities is known as "Net working capital"

Current Assets: One important current asset is accounts receivable. Accounts receivable arise because companies do not usually expect customers to pay for their purchases immediately. These unpaid bills are a valuable asset that companies expect to be able to turn into cash in the near future. The bulk of accounts receivable consists of unpaid bills from sales to other companies and are known as trade credit. The remainder arises from the sale of goods to the final consumer. These are known as consumer credit.

Another important current asset is inventory. Inventories may consist of raw materials, work in process, or finished goods awaiting sale and shipment.

In managing their cash companies face much the same problem you do. There are always advantages to holding large amounts of ready cash—they reduce the risk of running out of cash and having to borrow more on short notice. On the other hand, there is a cost to holding idle cash balances rather than putting the money to work earning interest.

In later we will tell you how the financial manager collects and pays out cash and decides on an optimal cash balance.

Current Liabilities: We have seen that a company's principal current asset consists of unpaid bills. One firm's credit must be another's debit. Therefore, it is not surprising that a company's principal current liability consists of *accounts payable*—that is, outstanding payments due to other companies. The other major current liability consists of short-term borrowing. We will have more to say about this later in this material.

4.1.3. Operating Cycle/Need for Working Capital

Every business needs some amount of working capital. The need for working capital arises due to the time gap between the production and realization of cash from sales. Thus working capital is needed for the following purposes:

1. For the purchase of raw material, components and spares parts.
2. To pay wages and salaries
3. To incur day-to-day expenses.
4. To meet the selling costs packing, advertising.
5. To provide the credit facilities to the customers.
6. To maintain the inventories of Raw material, work in progress, finished stock.

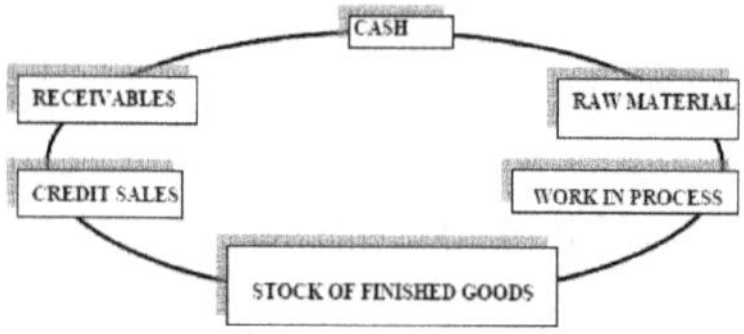

Working Capital/Operating Cycle of a Manufacturing Concern

There is an operating cycle involved in the sales and realization of cash. The cycle starts with the purchase of raw material and ends with the realization of cash from sales of finished foods. It involves purchase of raw material and stores, it conversion into stock of finished goods through work in progress, conversion of finished stock in to sales, debtors and receivables and ultimately in cash and this cycle continues again from cash to purchase of raw material and so on.

The gross operating cycle of the firm= RMCP+WIPCP+FGCP+RCP

Where,

RMCP= Raw Material conversion period

WIPCP= Work in progress conversion period

FGCP= Finished goods conversion period

RCP= Receivables conversion period.

However a firm may acquire some resources of credit and thus defer payments for certain period.

In this case,

Net operating cycle period= Gross operating cycle-payable deferral period.

Cash conversion cycle= (inventory period+ receivables period)- accounts payable period

The longer the production process, the more cash the firm must keep tied up in inventories. Similarly, the longer it takes customer to pay their bills, the higher the value of accounts receivables. On the other hand, if a firm can delay paying for its own materials, it may reduce the amount of cash it needs. In other words, accounts payable reduce net working capital.

Inventory period= Average Inventory/ Annual cost of goods sold/365

The denominator in this equation is the firms daily output. The ratio of inventory to daily output measures the average number of days from the purchase of the inventories to the final sale.

The accounts receivable period and the accounts payable period can be estimated in similar way:

Accounts receivable period= Average accounts receivable/ annual sales/365

Accounts payable period= Average accounts payable/annual cost of goods sold/365

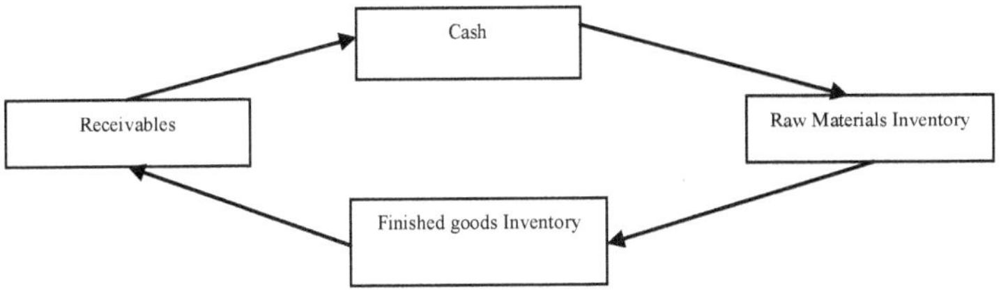

Simple Cycle of Operations

Calculation of Operating Cycle

1. Calculate the Stocking Period of the Raw Material

It is the time taken by the firm to convert raw material into semi-finished goods or work in process.

Stocking period= Average stock of raw material/Average daily consumption of raw material=n1 days.

Average stock of raw material= (opening stock + closing stock)/2

Average daily consumption= (annual consumption of raw material)/360

2. Calculation of Conversion Period of Raw Material into Finished Goods

It is the time taken by the firm to convert the work in process into finished goods.

Conversion period= Average work in process(WIP)/Average daily cost of production=n2 days

Average Work in process (WIP) = (opening stock + closing stock)/2

Average daily consumption= (annual consumption of raw material)/360

Annual cost of production=Opening stock of WIP+ consumption of RM+ other manufacturing costs – closing WIP.

3. Storage Period of Finished Goods

This is the time period required by the firm in converting finished goods.

Storage period= Average stock of finished goods/Average daily cost of sales =n3 days

Average stock of finished goods= (opening stock of Finished Goods+ closing stock of Finished Goods)/2

Average daily cost of sale=annual cost of sale/360

Annual cost of sales= opening stock of finished goods + cost of production + excise duty + selling and distribution expenses + general administrative costs - closing stock of finished goods.

4. Average Collection Period

This is the time taken by the debtors in paying the firm against credit sales.

Average collection period= Average sundry debtors/Average daily credit sales=n4 days

Average sundry debtors= (Opening debtors/Closing debtors)/2

Average daily credit sales= annual credit sale/360

5. *Average Payment Period of the Firm*

This is the time taken by the firm in paying its creditors against credit purchases.

Average payment period= Average balance of sundry creditors/average daily credit purchase=n5 days

Average balance of sundry creditors= (opening balance of creditors/closing creditors)/2

Average daily credit purchase=Annual credit purchase/360

Gross operating cycle period=n1+n2+n3+n4

Net operating cycle period=n+n2+n3+n4-n5

The gross operating cycle period is calculated by adding n1+n2+n3+n4 days. Where n1 denotes raw material storage period, n2 denotes conversion period of raw material into finished goods, n3 denotes the finished goods storage period before sales, and n4 denotes the average collection period for collecting accounts receivables. When n5 is subtracted from gross operating cycle one gets net operating cycle. Here n5 denotes the average payment period for making payment against accounts payable.

When operating cycle is of a short duration, it implies that funds that have been blocked in current assets are invested for a short time period. Thus the funds invested generate profit quickly.

Kinds of Working Capital

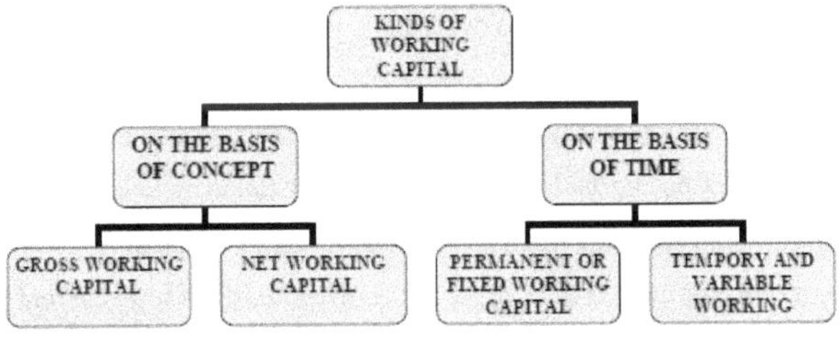

(a) On the Basis of Concept

(i) Gross working capital concept: According to this concept, working capital means total all of current assets of business.

(ii) Net working capital: According to this concept, working capital means excess of current assets over current liabilities.

Net Working capital= Current Assets- Current Liabilities.

As per the general practice net working capital is referred to simply as working capital

(b) On the Basis of Time

i. **Fixed or permanent working capital:** There is always a minimum level of current assets which is continuously required by the enterprise to carry out normal business operation. For Ex. Every firm has to maintain a minimum level of stock and cash balance. This minimum level of current assets is called fixed working capital as this amount is permanently blocked in current assets.

ii. **Temporary or Variable working capital:** It is that amount of working capital which is required to meet the seasonal demand and some special needs. Any amount over and above the permanent level of working capital is called as Temporary or variable working capital.

Types of Working Capital

(i) Permanent or Fixed Working Capital: It is the minimum amount of current assets required for conducting the business operation. This capital will remain permanent in current assets and should be financed out of long term funds. The amount varies from year to year, depending upon the growth of a company. The permanent (or) fixed working capital may be sub divided in the following: (a) Regular working capital and (b) Reserve margin (or) cushion working capital.

(ii) Temporary or variable working capital: It is the amount of additional current assets required for a short period. It is needed to meet the seasonal demands at different times during a year. It is temporary hence it should be financed out of short term funds. The working capital starts decreasing when the peak season is over. It may be sub divided into:

a. Seasonal working capital (capital required to meet seasonal needs)

b. Special working capital (required to meet special exigencies such as launching of extensive marketing campaigns, for conducting research etc)

(iii) Gross working capital: It is amount of funds invested in the total current assets.

(iv) Net working capital: It is excess of current assets over current liabilities.

(v) Negative or quantitative working capital: It occurs when current liabilities exceed current assets.

(vi) Positive or qualitative net working capital: It arises when current assets exceed current liabilities.

(vii) Reserve working capital: It refers to the short term financial arrangement made by the business units to meet uncertain changes or uncertainties.

Factors Influencing Working Capital

The need for working capital for day to day operations is influenced by number of factors. Some of the important factors are given below:

a. Nature of Business

Working capital depends upon the nature of business. Service oriented concerns like electricity, water supplies need limited working capital whereas manufacturing concerns require sufficient working capital, since they have to maintain stocks and debtors.

b. Credit Policies

A company which allows credit to its customers will need higher amount of higher amount of working capital. Likewise, a company enjoying credit facilities from its suppliers will need less amount of working capital.

c. Manufacturing Process

Manufacturing process involves conversion of raw materials into finished product. The longer the process, the higher the requirement of working capital. Therefore length of manufacturing process is one of the factors which influence the working capital requirements.

d. Changes in Technology

Changes in technology affect the requirement of working capital. If the firm adopts labour intensive process it requires more working capital. If it goes for automation, it improves the raw material processing, reducing the wastages and makes fast production. Hence the requirement of working capital is less.

e. Rapidity of Turnover

High rate of turnover requires low amount of working capital and lower and slow moving stock need a larger working capital. For example, slow moving jewellery shops have to maintain different types of jewellery shops have to maintain different types of jewellery which requires high working capital. But, high moving grocery shops require low working capital.

f. Business Cycle

Change in the economy also influences the working capital. When a business is prosperous, it requires huge amount of capital. Also during depression huge amount of working capital is required for unsold stock, uncollected debts.

g. *Seasonal Variation*

Industries which are manufacturing and selling goods seasonally require large amount of working capital.

h. *Fluctuation of Supply*

Firms have to maintain large reserves of raw materials in stores to avoid interrupted production, which requires large amount of working capital.

i. *Dividend Policy*

If a conservative dividend policy is followed by the management, the need for working capital can be met with the retained earnings. It consequently drains off large amounts from working capital pool.

Factors Determining Working Capital Requirements

The working capital requirement of a concern depends upon a large number of factors, which are as follows:

1. Nature or character of business: Public utility undertakings like Electricity, Water supply and Railways need very limited working capital because they offer cash sales only and supply services not products. On the other hand, Trading and Financial firms require less investment in fixed assets but have to investment large amount in current assets like inventories, receivables etc.
2. Size of business: Greater the size of business unit, generally larger will be the requirement of working capital. In some case even a smaller concern need more working capital due to high overhead charges, inefficient use of resources etc.
3. Production policy: The production could be kept either steady by accumulating inventories during slack periods with a view to meet high demand during the peak season or the production could be curtailed during the slack season and increased during peak season. If the policy is to keep the production steady by accumulating inventories it will require higher working capital.
4. Seasonal Variations: In certain industries, raw material; is not available throughout year. They have to buy raw material in bulk during the season to ensure an uninterrupted flow and process them during the entire year. A huge amount is blocked in the form on material inventories during such season, which give rise to more working capital.

5. Working capital cycle: In manufacturing concern, the working capital cycle starts with the purchase of raw material and ends with the realization of cash from the sales of finished products. This cycle involves purchase of raw material and starts, its conversion into stock of finished goods through work in progress with progressive increment of labor and service costs, conversion of finished stock into sales, Debtor and receivables and ultimately realization of cash and this cycle continues again from cash to purchase of raw material so on.
6. Rate of stock turnover: There is high degree of inverse co relationship between the quantum of working capital and the velocity or speed with which the sales are affected. A firm with having a high rate of stock turnover will need lower amount of working capital as compared to the firm having a low rate of turnover.
7. Credit policy: A Concern that purchases its requirement on credits and sells its products / services on cash requires lesser amount of working capital. On the other hand, concern buying its requirement for cash and allow credit to its customers, will need larger amount of working capital as very huge amount of funds are bound to be tied up in debtors or bills receivables.
8. Business Cycle: Business Cycle refers to alternate expansion and contraction in general business activity. In period of boom i.e. when the business is prosperous, there is need for larger amount of working capital due to increase in sales, rise in prices, and expansion of business. On the contrary in the times of depression i.e., when there is down swing of cycle, the business contracts, sales decline, difficulties are faced in collection from debtors and firms may have a large amount of working capital lying idle.
9. Rate of Growth of business: For the fast growing concern, larger amount of working capital is required.

Various approaches for determining the working capital financing mix:

There are three basic approaches for determining the working capital financing mix.

(i) The Hedging Approach

Under this approach, the maturity of source of funds should match the nature of assets to be financed. Therefore, it is also termed as "Matching Approach". It divides the requirements of total working capital funds into two categories viz. permanent working capital and temporary (or) seasonal working capital.

The permanent working capital requirements should be financed by long term funds while the seasonal working capital requirements should be financed out of short term funds. It results in high profit and high risk.

(ii) The Conservative Approach

According to this approach all requirements of funds should be met from long term sources. The short term sources should be used only for emergency requirements. The risk is low in this approach, so also the profit.

(iii) Trade-off Between Hedging and Conservative Approaches

Under this approach a tradeoff between hedging and conservative approaches is determined. One way of determining the level of trade off is by finding the average of the minimum and the maximum requirements of working capital during a period. The average working capital so obtained may be financed by long term funds and the balance by short term funds.

Procedure for Calculating Working Capital Forecasting

Forecasting the working capital requirement is a difficult problem faced by each businessman. The calculation of working capital requirements involves estimation of various components of current assets and current liabilities. The assessment can be:

a) Total quantity of units to be produced in a year.
b) Total costs incurred on materials, wages and overheads.
c) Length of time for which raw materials are kept in stores.
d) Length of the period during which finished product is kept in warehouse.
e) Credit allowed to debtors
f) Credit allowed to creditors
g) Lag in payment of wages and overheads.
h) Suitable adjustments to be made to provide for contingencies and seasonal factors.

4.1.4. Estimation of Working Capital Requirements

Factors Requiring Consideration while Estimating Working Capital

1. Total costs incurred on material, wages and overheads.
2. The length of the time for which materials are to remain in stores before they are issued for production.
3. The length of the production cycle or work in progress.

4. The length of the sales cycle during which finished goods are to be kept waiting for sales.
5. The average period of credit allowed to customers.
6. The amount of cash required to pay day to day expenses of the business.
7. The average amount of cash required to make the payments.
8. The average credit period expected to be allowed by suppliers.
9. Time lag in the payment of wages and other expenses.

Illus 1: The following information is taken from the books of a manufacturing concern; calculate the operating cycle in days:

Period covered	365 days
Average period of credit allowed by supplier	15 days
Average debtors outstanding	450
Raw materials consumption	4000
Total production cost	9500
Total cost of goods sold	10,000
Sales for the year	15,500
Value of average stock maintained:	
Raw materials	300
Work in progress	330
Finished goods	270

Solution

Raw material:

1. RMCP = Average Raw material/ Raw material consumed x365

   =300/4000*365=27 days
2. Work in progress

   WPCP= Average work in progress/ Total cost of production x 365

   =330/9500*365=12 days
3. Finished goods

   FGCP= Average finished goods/ Total cost of goods sold x 365

   =270/10000*365 = 9 days
4. Debtors

   RCP=Average debtors/credit sales x 365

   =450/15500*365=10 days

The average period of credit allowed by suppliers is 15 days

Therefore, Total operating cycle period:

=RMCP+WPCP+FGCP+DCP

=27+12+9+10

=58 days

Net Operating cycle:

= Total operating cycle period- Deferred period

=58-15

=43 days

This means that the firm has a net operating cycle of 34 days.

Illus 2: Davis Ltd has obtained the following data concerning the average working capital cycle for other companies in the same industry.

Raw material stock turnover	20 days
Credit received	40 days
Work In progress turnover	15 days
Finished goods stock turnover	40 days
Debtor's collection period	50 days

From the following data, calculate the current working capital cycle for Davis co. ltd.

	Rs.
Sales	3500
Cost of production	2000
Purchases	600
Average raw material	70
Average work in progress	85
Average finished goods	150
Average creditors	75
Average debtors	300

Solution

Computation of operating cycle of Davis Co. Ltd

1. Raw material = Average Raw Material/ Total Raw material *365

   = 70/600 *365 = **43 days**

2. Work in progress = Average work in progress/ Total cost of production *365

   = 85/2000*365 =**16 days**

3. Finished goods= Average stock/ Cost of production *365

   = 150/2000 *365 = **27 days**

4. Debtors= Average debtors/ Total Credit sales *365

   = 300/3500*365 =**31 days**

5. Creditors = Average creditors/Total Purchases *365

   = 75/600 * 365 =**45 days**

Net operating cycle = 43+16+27+31-45

= **72 days**

Illus: 3: From the following information, extracted from the books of a manufacturing company, compute the operating cycle in days and the amount of working capital required:

Period covered	365 days
Average period of credit allowed by suppliers	16 days
Average Total of debtors outstanding	Rs.480
Raw Material consumption	Rs.4,400
Total Production cost	Rs.10,000
Total Cost of Sales	Rs.10,500
Sales for the year	Rs.16,000
Value of Average Stock Maintained:	
Finished Goods	Rs.260
Raw Materials	Rs.320
Work-in-progress	Rs.350

Solution

Computation of Operating Cycle:

a) Raw materials held in stock:

   Average stocks of raw materials held/ Average consumption per day

   =320/4400/365

   =320*365/4400

   =27 days

   Less: Average credit period granted by suppliers =16 days

   =11 days

b) Work in progress:

   Average maintained/ Average cost of production per day

   =350/10000/365 =365*350/10,000=13 days

c) Finished goods held in stock

Average finished goods maintained / Average cost of goods sold per day

= 260/10500/365

=260*365/10500 = 9 days

d) Credit period allowed to debtors

Average total of outstanding debtors/Average credit sales per day

=480/16000/365

=365*480/16000= 11 days

Total Operating cycle period: (i) + (ii) +(iii) + (iv) = 44 days

Number of operating cycles in a year = 365/44 = 8.30

Amount of working capital required = Total operating cost/Number of operating cycles in a year

= 10,500/8.30 = Rs.1265

Alternatively, the amount of working capital could have also been calculated by estimating components of working capital method.

Illus: 4: From the following particulars prepare a statement showing working capital needed to finance a level of activity of 12,000 units of output per annum.

Analysis of selling price per unit.

	Rs.
Raw materials	5
Labour	3
Overhead	2
Total cost	10
Profit	2
Selling Price	12

Additional information:

a) Raw materials are to remain in store on an average- one month

b) Materials are in process, on an average – 2 months

c) Finished goods are in stock on an average – 3 months

d) Credit allowed to debtors is 4 months

e) Credit allowed by suppliers is 2 months

It may be assumed that production and overheads accrue evenly throughout the year.

Solution

Statement of working capital requirement

Particulars	Rs.	Rs.
Current Assets:		
a) Stock of Raw materials (1 month) (12000*5*12)		5000
b) Working in progress (2 months):		
Raw Materials (12000*5*2/12)	10000	
Labour (12000*3*2/12) *1/2 (See note iii)	3000	
Overheads (12000*2*2/12) *1/2 (See note iii)	2000	15000
c) Stock of finished goods (3 months) (12,000*10*3/12) (See note i)		30000
d) Debtors (4 months) (12,000*12*4/12) (See note i)		48000
		98000
Less: Current Liabilities: e) Creditors (2 months) Rs.5000*2		10000
Requirement of Working Capital		88000

Note: i) Stock is calculated on the basis of cost.

ii) Debtor is calculated on the basis of sales (Profit is not excluded)

iii) Wages and overhead accrue evenly through the year, when the production is in progress. Hence, the total cost of wages and overheads is become due for half the time on an average.

Illus: 5: From the following information, you are required to estimate the net working capital:

	Cost per unit
Raw materials	Rs.400
Direct Labour	Rs.150
Overheads (excluding depreciation)	Rs.300
Total cost	Rs.850

Additional information:

Selling price	Rs.1000 per unit
Output	52000 units
Raw materials in stock	average 4 weeks
Work in progress (assumed 50% completion stage with full material consumption)	average 2 weeks
Finished goods in stock	average 4 weeks
Credit allowed by suppliers	average 4 weeks
Credit allowed to debtors	average 8 weeks

Cash at bank is expected to be Rs.50,000

Assume that production is sustained at an even pace during the 52 weeks of the year. All sales are on credit basis.

Solution

Statement of Working Capital Requirement

Particulars	Rs.	Rs.
Current Assets:		
a) Stock of Raw materials (4 weeks) (52000*400*4/52)		16,00,000
b) Working in progress (2 weeks):		
Raw Materials (52000*400*2/52)	8,00,000	
Labour (52000*150*2/52) *50/100	1,50,000	
Overheads (52000*300*2/52) *50/100	3,00,000	12,50,000
c) Stock of finished goods (4 weeks) (52,000*850*4/52)		34,00,000
d) Debtors (8 weeks) (52,000*1000*52)		80,00,000
		1,42,50,000
Less: Current Liabilities:		
f) Creditors (4 weeks) (5000*400*4/52)		16,00,000
		1,26,50,000
Add: Cash at Bank		50,000
Net Working Capital requirements		1,27,00,000

Illus: 6: A company sells goods in the home market and earns a gross profit of 20% on sales. Its annual figures are as follows:

Sales	Rs.3,00,000
Materials used	Rs.1,08,000
Wages	Rs.96,000
Manufacturing expenses	Rs.1,20,000
Administrative expenses	Rs.30,000
Depreciation	Rs.12,000
Selling expenses	Rs.18,000

Income tax payable in two installments of which one falls in the next year Rs.30000

Additional information:

1. Credit given by suppliers - 2months
2. Credit allowed to customers - 1 month
3. Lag in payment of wages - ½ month
4. Selling expenses are paid quarterly in advance.

5. Raw materials and finished goods are in stock for 1month.
6. Cash balance estimated to be maintained at Rs.30,000.

You are required to prepare a statement of working capital requirements.

Solution

Statement of Working Capital Requirements

Particulars	Rs.
Current Assets:	
Stock of Raw materials (1 Month) Rs.1,08,000*1/12	9000
*Stock of finished goods (1 Month) Rs. 2,40,000*1/12	20,000
Prepaid selling expenses (3 Months) Rs.18,000*3/12	4,500
* Debtors (1 Month) Rs.2,40,000*1/12	20,000
Cash balance to be maintained	30,000
Current Assets	83,500
Less: Current Liabilities:	
Sundry creditor (2 Months) Rs.1,08,000*2/12	18,000
Lag in payment of wages (1/2 Month) Rs.96,000 *0.5/12	4,000
Lag in payment of Manufacturing expenses (1 Month) Rs.1,20,000*1/12	10,000
Current Liabilities	32,000
Requirement of Working Capital (CA-CL)	51,500

Working:

a) Sales Rs.3,00,000

Less: Gross profit (20% on sales) Rs. 60,000

Cost of Sales Rs.2,40,000

b) Depreciation is a non-cash item. Hence, it will not affect the working capital statement.

c) Income tax payable is related to the next financial year. So, it will not appear in the working capital statement of the current year.

d) Stock of finished goods and Debtors are calculated on cost of sales.

Illus: 6: You are required to prepare a statement showing the working capital required to finance the level of activity of 18,000 units per year from the following information:

Particulars	**Rs.**
Raw material Per Unit	12
Direct labor Per Unit	3
Overheads per Unit	9
Total cost Per Unit	24
Profit per Unit	6
Selling price Per Unit	30

Additional Information

1. Raw material is in stock on an average for 2 months.
2. Materials are in process on an average for half-a- month.
3. Finished goods are in stock on an average for two months.
4. Credit allowed by creditors is two months in respect of raw materials supplied.
5. Credit allowed to debtors is three months.
6. Lag in payment of wages is half month. Cash on hand and at bank is expected to be Rs. 7,000.
7. You are informed that all activities are evenly spread out during the year.

Solution

Estimation of Working Capital

Current Assets:		Rs.
1. Stock-in-Trade		
a. Raw materials	$18{,}000 \times 12 \times \frac{2}{12}$ =	36,000
b. Work in progress	$18000 \times 18 \times \frac{½}{12}$ =	13,500
c. Finished goods	$18{,}000 \times 24 \times \frac{2}{12}$ =	72,000
		1, 21,500
2. Sundry debtors	$18{,}000 \times 30 \times \frac{3}{12}$ =	1, 35,000
3. Cash on hand and at bank	$18{,}000 \times 30 \times \frac{3}{12}$ =	7,000
		2, 63,500
Less: Current liabilities		
4. Sundry creditors	$18{,}000 \times 12 \times \frac{3}{12}$ =	36,000
5. Wages	$18{,}000 \times 3 \times \frac{½}{12}$ =	2250
Estimated Working Capital Requirement		2, 25,250

Working Notes

(1) Cost of each unit of Work in process Rs.

Raw materials 12

Labour (50% of Rs. 3) 1.50

Overhead(50% of Rs. 9) 4.50

Total 18

Illus:7: Runwall Ltd. had annual sales of 50,000 units at Rs.100per unit. The company works for 50 weeks in the year. Cost details of the Company are as given below:

Particulars	**Rs.**
Raw material Per Unit	30
Labour Per Unit	10
Overheads per Unit	20
Total cost Per Unit	60
Profit per Unit	40
Selling price Per Unit	100

Additional Information

1. The Company has the practice of storing raw materials for 4weeks requirements.
2. The wages and other expenses are paid after a lag of 2 weeks.
3. Further the debtors enjoy a credit of 10 weeks and Company gets a credit of 4 weeks from suppliers.
4. The processing time is 2 weeks and finished goods inventory is maintained for 4 weeks.
5. From the above information prepare a working capital estimate, allowing for a 15% Contingency.

Solution

Estimation working Capital:

Current Assets:		Rs.
1. Stock-in-Trade		
a. Raw materials	$50{,}000 \times 30 \times \frac{4}{50}$ =	1, 20,000
b. Work in progress	$50{,}000 \times 45 \times \frac{2}{50}$ =	90,000
c. Finished goods	$50{,}000 \times 60 \times \frac{4}{50}$ =	2, 40,000
		4, 50,000
2. Sundry debtors	$50{,}000 \times 100 \times \frac{10}{50}$ =	10, 00,000
		14, 50,000

Less: Current liabilities:

3. Sundry creditors	$50,000 \times 30 \times \frac{4}{50}$ =	1, 20,000
4. Wages	$50,000 \times 10 \times \frac{2}{50}$ =	20,000
1. Overhead	$50,000 \times 20 \times \frac{2}{50}$ =	40,000
		12, 70,000
Add: 10 % for contingencies		1, 27,000
Estimated Working Capital Requirement		13, 97,000

Working Notes:

(1) Cost of each unit of Work in process	Rs.
Raw materials	30
Labour (50% of Rs. 10)	5
Overhead (50% of Rs. 20)	10
Total	45

4.2. Accounts Receivables Management

Accounts receivable management incorporates is all about ensuring that customers pay their invoices. Good receivables management helps prevent overdue payment or non-payment. It is therefore a quick and effective way to strengthen the company's financial or liquidity position.

Accounts receivable represent the amount due form customers (book debts) or debtors as a result of selling goods on credit. "The term debtors is defined as 'debt' owned to the firm by customers arising from sale of goods or services in the ordinary course of business." The three characteristics of receivables the element of risk, economic value and futurity explain the basis and the need for efficient management of receivables. The element of risk should be carefully analyzed. Cash sales are totally riskless but not the credit sales, as the same has yet to be received. To the buyer the economic value in goods and services process immediately at the time of sale, while the seller expect an equivalent value to be received later on. The cash payment for goods and services received by the buyer will be made by him in a future period. The customer from whom receivables or book debts have to be collected in future are called Trade debtor and represent the firm's claim on assets.

Receivables management, also termed as credit management, deals with the formulation of credit policy, in terms of liberal or restrictive, concerning credit standard and credit period, the discount offered for early payment and the collection policy and procedures undertaken. It does so in such a way that taken together these policy variables determine an optimal level of investment in receivables where the return on that investment is maximum to the firm. The credit period extended by business firm usually ranges from 15 to 60 days. When goods are sold on credit, finished goods get converted into accounts receivable (trade debtors) in the books of the seller. In the books of the buyer, the obligation arising from credit purchase is represented as accounts payable (trade creditors). "Accounts receivable is the total of all credit extended by a firm to its customer."

A firm's investment in account receivable depends upon how much it sells on credit and how long it takes to collect receivable. Accounts receivable (or sundry debtors) constitute the 3rd most important assets category for business firm after plant and equipment and inventories and also constitute the 2nd most important current assets category for business firm after inventories.

Poor management of accounts receivables are: neglect of various overdue account, sharp rise in the bad debt expense, and the collection of debts expense and taking the discount by customers even though they pay after the discount date and even after the net date. Since accounts receivable represent a sizable investment on the part of most firms in the case of public enterprises in India it forms 16 to 20 per cent of current assets. Efficient management of these accounts can provide considerable saving to the firm.

Factors involving in Receivable management:

1. The terms of credit granted to customers deemed creditworthy.
2. The policies and practices of the firm in determining which customers are to be granted credit.
3. The paying practices of credit customers.
4. The vigoir of the sellers, collection policies and practice.
5. The volume of credit sales.

Credit Policy

The first stage of credit sales is to decide policy in which most important variable is whether credit sales should be made or not and if yes to what extent i.e. what percentage of sales should be done on cash and what percentage on credit. The discussion with cement companies marketing and financé department clearly suggest that the credit policy is more dependent upon market forces and less on company specially in periods when there is excessive competition which has happened a number of times in the history of cement industry after decontrol and manufactures have been forced to provide credit if they wanted full utilization of capacity. If in the market there is practice of providing credit, those companies who do not fall in line have lower sales and so lower utilization of instilled capacity. The management has to weigh whether it should avoid risk of realization and problem of arranging funds for larger sales on credit or decide for reduced capacity utilization thereby resulting in higher cost per tonne of cement produced.

Actually the policy should be based on cost benefit analysis of these factors but often policy is decided without detailed calculations. In actual practice when one waits to push sales the marketing department pressurizes the management to provide liberal credit to buyers to realize sales targets.

Credit Rating

The second virtual point of credit policy is to whom to give credit and whom it should be denied. Whether it should be given to everyone or on selective basis? As per standards one can workout impact of credit sales on profits by following formulae:

$\Delta P = \Delta S\ (1\text{-}V) - K * \Delta I - B, \Delta S$

in the above formula

ΔP = Change in profit

ΔS = Change in sales

V = Ratio of variable cost to sales

K = Cost of capital i.e. interest cost of credit

ΔI = Increase in receivables investment

B = Bad debts ratio on additional sales

The change in profits (ΔP) is dependent upon ratio of variable cost and fixed cost and change in sales. The figure is worked out by deducting variable cost from sales i.e. sales minus variable cost is change in profits.

The above formula appears to be very simple but for policy purposes it requires that policy maker should be able to estimate precisely the impact of credit on sales value, the variable cost and bad debts besides the cost of capital. In practice besides the cost of capital, it is very difficult to measure extent of increase in sales as a result of credit and it is only broad estimate of sales department. Similarly, it is very difficult if not impossible to workout likely bad debts. The variable cost can be worked out with great precision if proper costing system is maintained. Because of difficulties in quantifying various variables in the formulae often credit policy is decided without working details on prevailing market conditions and the need of the company to push sales at a point of time. It has been by various companies that no details are worked.

Credit Period

The credit period is the time length for which seller agrees to provide credit to the buyers. It varies according to the practice of trade and varies between 15 to 60 days. In some cases for an early payment pre-agreed discount is given to induce buyer make an early payment. For late payment in the agreement there is provision for interest payment by buyer. If credit is given for longer period it induces to push up sales but this is true only when one provides longer period credit than competitors. The customer-distributor, dealer, consumers is attracted to a firm who provides longer period credit. The impact of credit on profits and sales can be worked out from the following formula:

$\Delta P= \Delta S\ (1-V)*K*\Delta 1-b, \Delta S$

The various components are as under :

Δ P= Change in profit

Δ S= Change in sales

Δ 1= Change in investments receivables

V= Ratio of variable cost to sales

K= Cost of giving credit

b= bad debits ratio to increased credit

The discussion with the industry suggests that they rarely take decision on period of credit based on formula. It is market conditions and practices in the trade, which decides the period of credit and hardly any calculations of cost are done. In practice it is marketing department whose advice plays an important and deciding role. In the period when sales have to be pushed up more credit is provided and there is no uniform policy overtime. During rainy season (July-Sep.) when demand is generally slack more liberal credit is granted than rest of the year. Further, when stocks accumulate due to sluggish sales, producers accept the terms of their customers and traders about the period of credit but when market conditions are tight, the seller becomes more strict in providing credit.

4.3. Factoring

Factoring is similar to breaking up a number into its multiples. For example, 10=5*2. The multiples are '5' and '2'. In a polynomial it is the same way, however, the procedure is somewhat more complicated since variables, not just numbers, are involved. There are different ways of factoring an equation depending on the complexity of the polynomial.

Factoring by Grouping

There will be occasions when there are no common factors for all terms, but there will be terms that have a variable in common while other terms have a different variable in common. In this case, we can factor by grouping together these common terms.

4.4. Inventory Management

In the supply chain one of the key variables which has to be managed is inventory. The inventory includes a vast spectrum of materials that is being transferred, stored, consumed, produced, packaged, or sold in one way or another during a firm`s normal course of business.

- The planning, storing, moving and accounting for inventory is the basis for all logistics
- Inventory has a financial value, which for accounting purposes is considered a floating asset. However, it may be very difficult to convert physical inventory into liquid assets, hence the inventory is very risky investment
- Inventories represent the largest single investment in assets form many manufacturers, wholesalers and retailers. Inventory investment represents over 20% of the total assets of manufacturers and more than 50% of the total assets of wholesalers and retailers
- Thus one goal in operations is to keep the level of inventory in the supply chain as to low as possible thus freeing up funds for other purposes.
- Holding the inventories is connected with significant costs. Despite the all efforts and technological innovations, inventories are often still the asset with lowest return in the company. Arguably majority of companies hold 25-40% more inventories than actually needed. Unreasonably high inventory levels lower the company`s profit and return of assets.

Reasons for Inventories

- Improve customer service

  Provides immediacy in product availability

- Encourage production, purchase, and transportation economies
  Allows for long production runs
  Takes advantage of price-quantity discounts
  Allows for transport economies from larger shipment sizes
- Act as a hedge against price changes
  Allows purchasing to take place under most favorable price terms
- Protect against uncertainties in demand and lead times
  Provides a measure of safety to keep operations running when demand levels and lead times cannot be known for sure
- Act as a hedge against contingencies
  Buffers against such events as strikes, fires, and disruptions in supply

Reasons against Inventories

- They consume capital resources that might be put to better use elsewhere in the firm
- They too often mask quality problems that would more immediately be solved without their presence
- They divert management's attention away from careful planning and control of the supply and distribution channels by promoting an insular attitude about channel management

Effective Inventory Management

Effective inventory management is the result of outstanding inventory control and inventory management.

- Inventory control involves managing the inventory that is already in the warehouse, stockroom or store. That is knowing, what products are "out there", have much you have each item and where it is. It means having accurate , complete and timely inventory transactions record and avoiding differences between accounting and real inventory levels. Two tools commonly employed to ensure inventory accuracy and control are ABC analysis and cycle counting
- Inventory management involves determining, how to order products and how much to order as well as identifying the most effective source of supply for each item in each stocking location. Inventory management includes all activities of planning, forecasting and replenishment. The main purpose of inventory management is minimization differences between customers demand and availability of items. These

differences have caused by three factors: customers demand fluctuations, suppliers delivery time fluctuations and inventory control accuracy

Inventory Transactions

- Normal stock receipt – from previously issued purchase orders and transfers
- Unexpected stock receipts – the stuff that just shows up on receiving stock
- Requisitions – a request for material to be consumed within company
- Emergency requisitions
- Sales

  Orders to be delivered

  Orders to be picked up

  Cash sales

  Direct shipments

  Orders for non-stock products
- Transfers to other warehouses or facilities
- Assembly orders
- Bin to bin transfers within warehouse
- Returns of stock material
- Returns of non stock material
- Returns of damaged material
- Returns to supplier
- Adjustments of on-hand quantities – who is allowed to approve adjustments? Under what circumstances?
- Scrapping and writing-off stock

4.5. Cash Management

In 1981, President Ronald Reagan, OMB, and the President's Private Sector Survey on Cost Control said that the Federal Government could save a great deal of money by managing Federal cash as carefully as businesses manage their cash. Essentially, most Federal agencies concentrated on operating their programs and ignored the time-value of money. The President's Management Improvement Program took aim at reforming Federal financial management by making one of its top priorities the cessation of the needless loss of interest on cash flows. In 1981-82, a portion of the President's Management Improvement Program, Reform '88, was developed as a comprehensive program to improve, consolidate, and streamline the management systems of the Federal Government by a target date of 1988.

Reform '88 put new life into the management of Federal cash. Each Federal agency was required to monitor its own cash flows, selecting the best tools for speeding collections to the Treasury and timing disbursements to vendors, grantees, and other payment recipients. Before 1982, the U.S. Government made 30 percent of its payments too late and 45 percent too early, resulting in unnecessary late charges and lost interest earnings. Congress passed the Prompt Payment Act of 1982 (and its amendment in 1988) requiring Federal agencies to make payments on time, to pay interest when payments are late, and to take discounts only when payments are made on or before the discount date. It also provides a formula for determining if a discount is cost-effective. OMB wrote the regulations to implement the Prompt Payment Act, which provides for timely payment, better relations with contractors, improved competition for Government business, and reduced costs to the Government. Once the necessary legislation and regulations were in place to improve Federal agency management of payments, the Government turned its focus on collections. Congress passed the Deficit Reduction Act of 1984. A section of the Act, referred to generally as the Collection and Deposit Legislation, moved agencies closer to the goal of institutionalizing cash management in the Federal Government. It legislated cash management for collections and deposits analogous to the directives given to Federal agencies about paying their bills on time in the Prompt Payment Act of 1982. The Collection and Deposit Legislation mandated that the Treasury would hold Federal agencies responsible for their collection and deposit practices. Federal agencies must use electronic transfer of funds, lockboxes, and automatic withdrawal of funds wherever feasible and in accordance with Treasury regulations.

CHAPTER 5

LONG TERM SOURCES OF FINANCE

5.1. Indian Capital and Stock Market

5.1.1. The Role of the Indian Capital Market

The capital market in India is a market for securities, where companies and governments can raise long term funds. It is a market designed for the selling and buying of stocks and bonds. Stocks and bonds are the two major ways to generate capital and long term funds. Thus, the bond markets and stock markets are considered as capital markets. The capital markets consist of the primary market, where new issues are distributed to investors, and the secondary market, where existing securities are traded. In addition, the Indian Equity Markets and the Indian Debt markets do form part of the Indian Capital market. The Indian Equity Market depends mainly on monsoons, global funds flowing into equities and the performance of various companies. The Indian Equity Market is almost wholly dominated by two major stock exchanges -National Stock Exchange of India Ltd. (NSE) and The Bombay Stock Exchange (BSE). The benchmark indices of the two exchanges - Nifty of NSE and Sensex of BSE are closely monitored by the investors. The two exchanges also have an F and O (Futures and options) segment for trading in equity derivatives including the indices. The major players in the Indian Equity Market are Mutual Funds, Financial Institutions and FIIs representing mainly Venture Capital Funds and Private Equity Funds. The Indian Equity Market at present is a lucrative field for investors. The Indian stocks are profitable not only for long and medium-term investors, but also for the position traders, short-term swing traders and also very short term intra-day traders and speculators. In India as on December 30 2007, market capitalisation (BSE 500) at US$ 1638 billion was 150 per cent of GDP, matching well with other emerging economies and selected matured markets. In a developing economy like India, the debt markets are very important sources of raising capital funds. The debt markets in India are amongst the largest in Asia. Their dealings included government securities, public sector undertakings, other government bodies, financial institutions, banks and companies. The debt markets play a role of increasing funds for implementation of government development plans. This means that government can raise funds at lower costs by issuing government securities. They are very conducive for the proper implementation of government's monetary policy. They provided a less risky investment environment compared to the equity markets, encouraging low-risk investments. This leads to foreign inflow of funds into the economy. They provide high liquidity and proper control over credit. They provided opportunity for investors to diversify their investment portfolio in a way to minimize risk. They promoted very stringent disclosure norms and auditing requirements, hence there was improved transparency and better implementation of corporate governance principles.

Members of the Indian Capital Markets

In order function properly the Indian capital markets operate through the following entities:

a. India Capital Markets Pvt. Ltd.- Members NSE, BSE and NSDL, ICM Commodities Pvt Ltd. – Members MCX, NCDEX
b. SEBI Registered PMS

The Functions and Main Institutions of the Indian Capital Market

(1) The functions of the Indian Capital Market are as Follows

i. Disseminate information efficiently for enabling participants to develop an informed opinion about investment, disinvestments, reinvestment, or holding a particular financial asset.
ii. Enabling quick valuation of financial instruments-both equity and debt.
iii. Providing insurance against market risk or price risk through derivative trading and default risk through investment protection fund.
iv. Enable wider participation by enhancing the width of the market by encouraging participation through networking institutions and associating individuals.
v. Provide operational efficiency through:
    (a) simplified transaction procedure
    (b) lowering settlement timings, and
    (c) lowering transaction costs
vi. Develop integration among
    (a) Real sector and financial sector
    (b) Equity and debt instruments
    (c) Long-term and short-term funds
    (d) Long-term and short-term interest costs
    (e) Private sector and government sector, and
    (f) Domestic funds and external funds
vii. Direct the flow of funds into efficient channels through investment, disinvestments, and reinvestment

(2) The Main Members of the Indian Capital Market

The capital market aids economic growth by mobilizing the savings o the economic sectors and directing the same towards channels of productive uses. This is facilitated through the following:

a) The Industrial Financial Corporation of India (IFC)
b) The Industrial Credit and Investment Corporation of India (ICICI)
c) The Refinance Corporation of India (RFC)
d) The State Financial Development Corporations (SFCs)
e) National Industrial Development Corporation (NIDC)
f) The State Industrial Development Corporation (SIDCs)
g) National Small Industries Corporation (NSIC)
h) Industrial Development Bank of India (IDBI)
i) Life Insurance Corporation of India (LIC)
j) Nationalized Commercial Banks (NCBs)
k) Merchant Banking Institutions (MBIs)
l) National Industrial Reconstruction Corporation of India (NIRC)
m) The Credit Guarantee Corporation of India (CGC)
n) Unit Trust of India (UTI).
o) These members are mainly financial institutions which provide the liquidity that is needed to propel the machinery of the Capital Market. The financial power of the Capital Market is in their hands. SEBI has the responsibility to oversee their proper functioning as well as the other members.

(3) Products and Services of the Capital Market

a. Equity Broking - BSE and NSE
b. Derivatives Futures and Options
c. Internet Broking- Online Trading
d. Commodities Trading - NCDEX and MCX
e. Mutual Fund Investment
f. Initial Public Offerings (IPO)
g. Institutional Broking
h. Depository Services - NSDL and CDSL
i. Portfolio Management Services
j. NRI Investments
k. Arbitrage

The Development in Indian Capital Market Since 1992

Capital Issues (Control) Act of 1947 repealed and the office of Controller of Capital Issues abolished; control over price and premium of shares removed. Companies now free to raise funds from securities markets after filing prospectus with the Securities and Exchange Board of India (SEBI).

The power to regulate Stock Exchanges delegated to SEBI by the Government. This was for better implementation of all reforms formulated and implemented to enable the proper functioning of the Stock Exchanges.

SEBI introduces regulations for primary and other secondary market intermediaries, bringing them within the regulatory framework.

Regulatory Framework for the Primary Market

The regulatory framework for primary markets in Indian comprises of the SEBI Act, 1992. SEBI regulations and rules for various intermediaries, for the issue of capital by management tie up with certain provisions of the companies Act, 1956. The following are the important enactments relating to the primary market in India (Table 4.1):

Table 5.1: Enactments Relating to the Indian Primary Market

Serial	Details
a	SEBI (Disclosure and Investor Protection) Guidelines, 2000
b	SEBI (Merchant Bankers) Rules and Regulations, 1992
c	SEBI (Banker to the Issue) Rules and Regulations, 1994
d	SEBI (Registrar to an Issue) Rules and Regulations, 1993
e	SEBI (Underwriters) Rules and Regulations, 1993

Source: SEBI (2008)

Primary Market Reforms

For the fulfillment of the basic task of Securities Market to help in process of capital formation in the economy, this can only be possible by series of systematic measures which would build their confidence in the systems and processes and protect their interest fully. The raising of Capital Issues was controlled by the office of the Controller of Capital Issues (CCI) established under the Capital Issues Control Act-1947.

The Capital Issues Control Act-1947 was repealed and the office of the controller of Capital Issues abolished and the process of the initial share pricing decontrolled. In 1991-92 the Finance Ministry announced the repeal of the Act and transferred all powers from CCI to SEBI and from control to disclosure based regulations.

SEBI, the Capital Market Regulator, was established in 1992. The primary function of SEBI is to regulate the Capital Market and protect the interest of the investors. The other important functions of SEBI are:

1. Regulating the business in Stock Exchanges and any other Securities Markets.
2. Registering and regulating the working of collective investment schemes, including mutual funds.
3. Prohibiting fraudulent and unfair trade practices relating to Securities Markets.

Therefore SEBI formulated the following guidelines:

a. Disclosure and Investor Protection (DIP) guidelines: as per this regulation all the information pertaining to and available with an issuer is provided so as the investor takes an informed decision whether to invest or not to invest.
b. Eligibility Criteria for issuers (DIP-2000): Companies eligible to make an issue can decide on their standard denomination and price of a security. Some parameters that need to be in offer documents are minimum holding by promoters, size of public issue, issue expenses, information disclosure and advertisement etc.
c. Transparency: SEBI makes available all the offer documents filed with it on its website and also through process release. Companies are invited from the public within 21 days of filing.
d. Free Pricing of Securities: issuer is free to determine the level of security price. The process of Book-building helps discover price and assist small investor to take an investment decision.
e. Number of Financial Instruments: issuer would like to have an optimum capital structure that reduces cost of capital. Today Indian Capital Market consists of almost all financial products available in most of the developed Capital Market, thus the choice to both issuer and investor has become wider.
f. Issue process: the following process is used in the Indian Capital Market:
    i. Public issue – an invitation by a company to the public to subscribe to the securities offered through prospects. It is an Initial Public Offer (IPO).
    ii. Rights Issue - issue of capital under Sec-I (81) Companies Act 1956 to be offered to existing shareholders.
    iii. Offer for Sale - It is a public invitation by a sponsoring intermediary, such as bank or broker, to buy new or existing securities. It contrasts with an offer for subscription which is an invitation to subscribe direct from the issuer.

iv. Book-building - it refers to a process of ascertaining demand for and price of securities through bids, before the Actual issue. Book building process is mandatory when the company does not have track record for three out of preceding five years. 60% allotment to qualified institutional buyers is mandatory under the book building process.

v. Compulsory Demat - All Initial public offerings was compulsory traded in dematerialized form. But the investors have been allowed to exercise option of either subscribing to securities in its physical or dematerialized form.

vi. Employee stock option – means option given to the whole time employee of a company right to purchase or subscribe securities at a future date.

vii. Buy-back – section 77 (A) Companies Act and SEBI regulation allow companies to buy back shares to enhance the wealth of shareholder.

g. Prohibiting insider trading in securities, with the imposition of monetary penalties, on defaulter market intermediaries.

h. Foreign Institutional Investors are allowed to invest in Indian Capital Markets after registration with the SEBI.

i. Indian companies permitted to access international Capital Markets through Euro issues.

j. The National Stock Exchanges, (NSE) with nationwide stock trading and electronic display, clearing and settlement facilities, established several regional Stock Exchanges change over from floor based grading to screen based trading.

k. Private Mutual Funds permitted.

l. The practice of making preferential allotment of shares at prices unrelated to the prevailing market prices stopped and fresh guidelines are issued by SEBI.

m. Badla System was been abolished.

n. A system of rolling settlements introduced and SEBI is thinking about the introduction of T+1 settlement plan for the Capital Market

The SEBI (credit rating Agencies) Regulations, 1999 issued for regulating new credit rating agencies as well as introducing a code of conduct for all credit rating agencies operating in India.

Further Primary Market Reforms

i. The improved disclosure standards, introduction of prudential norms, and simplification of issue procedures.

ii. Companies required disclosing all material facts and specific risk factors associated with their projects while making public issues.

iii. Listing agreements of stock exchanges amended to require listed companies to furnish annual statement to the exchanges showing variations between financial projections and projected utilization of funds in the offer document and actual figures. This is to enable shareholders to make comparisons between performance and promises.

iv. SEBI introduces a code of advertisement for public issues to ensure fair and truthful disclosures.

v. Disclosure norms further strengthened by introducing cash flow statements.

vi. New issue procedures introduced—book building for institutional investors—aimed at reducing costs of issuing shares.

vii. SEBI introduces regulations governing substantial acquisition of shares and takeovers and lays down conditions under which disclosures and mandatory public offers are to be made to the shareholders.

Regulations Further Revised and Strengthened in 1996

i. SEBI reconstitutes the governing boards of the stock exchanges and introduces capital adequacy norms for broker accounts.

ii. Private mutual funds permitted and several such funds already set up. All mutual funds allowed to apply for firm allotment in public issues—also aimed at reducing issue costs.

Regulations for Mutual Funds Revised in 1996

a. The giving of more flexibility to fund managers while increasing transparency, disclosure, and accountability.

b. Over-the-Counter Exchange of India formed.

c. National Stock Exchange (NSE) establishment as a stock exchange with nationwide electronic trading.

d. Bombay Stock Exchange (BSE) introduces screen-based trading; 15 stock exchanges now have screened-based trading. BSE granted permission to expand its trading network to other centres.

e. The Capital adequacy requirements for brokers enforced.

f. The System of mark-to-market margins introduced in the Stock Exchanges.

g. The stock lending scheme introduced.

h. Transparency brought out in short selling.

i. National Securities Clearing Corporation, Ltd. set up by National Stock Exchange.

j. Bombay Stock Exchange in the process of implementing a trade guarantee scheme.

k. SEBI strengthens surveillance mechanisms and directs all stock exchanges to have separate surveillance departments.

Secondary Market Reforms

Several reforms were introduced into the Stock Exchange administration, security trading, settlement, delivery Vs Payment, security transfer, trading in derivatives, investor protection fund etc. are explained in the following paragraphs:

(a) Stock Exchanges

Membership of governing boards of Stock Exchanges, were changed to include 50% outside (non-broker) representatives. SEBI had constituted a group which reviewed and examined the structure of Stock Exchanges and examined the legal and financial issues involved in demutualising Stock Exchanges.

(b) Depth and Breadth in the Market

India has a unique distinction of having highest number of companies listed on the Stock Exchanges. But all companies' shares are not traded. Policy makers have to explore new options to increase depths and breadth in the Indian Stock Exchanges.

(c) Dematerialization

Power was granted to SEBI to register and regulate depositories and custodians through an amendment to SEBI Act in 1995. There has been substantial progress in dematerialization. Number of companies available for demat with NSDL has increased from 23 in 1997 to 4172 in 2002.

(d) Institutionalization

The Indian Capital Market was dominated by individual investors, till the early part of the 1990's. Earlier institutional investors like LIC, GIC, DFIs, banks etc. used to take minor roles. SEBI permitted private funds, Non-resident Indians, NBFCs and overseas corporate bodies to trade in securities. Of the above mentioned, only three classes of investors are very active, individuals, mutual funds and FIIs.

(e) Development of Financial Infrastructure

It involves the development of informed investor class, legal and regulatory environment, institutional investors, world class security trading and payment and settlement systems. It also includes promoting investor associations, self-regulatory organizations (SROs), and setting up of depository's surveillance system. As another step towards this, SEBI has introduced new financial instruments (derivatives) into the Capital Market.

(f) Derivatives

Derivatives are financial contracts, or financial instruments, whose prices are derived from the price of something else (known as the underlying). The underlying price on which a derivative is based can be that of an asset (e.g., commodities, equities (stocks), residential mortgages, commercial real estate, loans, bonds), an index (e.g., interest rates, exchange rates, stock market indices, consumer price index (CPI), or other items. Credit derivatives are based on loans, bonds or other forms of credit. Futures and options belong to the family of derivative financial products. The name is coined from the fact that the price of these products can be derived from the price of a so called underlying product. Derivative products of BSE are futures and options contracts. These can play a vital role in promoting market efficiency through better price discovery and risk transfer. SEBI granted approval to NSE and BSE to start trading in index futures contract in April 2000 and May 2000 respectively. SEBI also approved the proposal of NSE and BSE to start trading in index options contracts in June 2001.

The Birth of the Scam

During the late nineteen eighties, the share mania spread, so rapidly that a lot more Stock Exchanges came into existence and the Indian Capital Market witnessed a hectic boom in the primary market activities with a number of existing and new companies floating issues. The number of companies getting listed on the bourses increased steadily. Investment and trading got to such a feverish pace that it gave birth to a major scam in the secondary market in 1992, (the Harshad Mehta scam of the early 1990s). The Indian Stock Exchange Index (Sensex), which was hovering around the 800 mark in early 1990, flared up past 3500 by April 1992 and plummeted. The Securities and Exchange Board of India (SEBI) that was formed in 1988 to look after the interests of small investors and to monitor the functioning of the bourses was accorded more powers following the scam that shook the market and sent many investors and brokers out of the ring.

It is clear that the government, the RBI and the commercial banks are as much accountable as the brokers for the scam. The brokers were encouraged and abetted by the banks to divert funds from the banking system to the stock market. The banks received very high interest rates for doing so, putting the investors at risk. The RBI stands indicted, because despite knowledge about banks over-stepping the boundaries demarcating their arena of operations, it failed to apply the necessary controls required at the time to deter the scam. The undesirable charging of very high interest rate by banks was done with active connivance and sometimes the full knowledge of the very individuals who were supposed to guard against such a possibility. The major scams in India from 1990 to 2009 have many namely:

(a) Ramalinga Raju Scam

The biggest corporate scam (January 2009) in India comes from one of the most respected businessmen. Satyam founder Byrraju Ramalinga Raju resigned as its chairman after admitting to cooking up the accounting books. His efforts to fill the "fictitious assets with real ones" through Maytas acquisition failed, after which he decided to confess the crime. With a fraud involving about Rs 8,000 crore (Rs 80 billion), Satyam is heading for more trouble in the future. In the event of this information the company lost a staggering Rs 10,000 crore (Rs 100 billion) in market capitalisation as investors reacted sharply and dumped shares, pushing down the scrip by 78 per cent to Rs 39.95 on the Bombay Stock Exchange.

(b) Harshad Mehta Scam

He was known as the 'Big Bull'. However, his bull run did not last too long. He triggered a rise in the Bombay Stock Exchange in the year 1992 by trading in shares at a premium across many segments. Taking advantages of the loopholes in the banking system, Harshad and his associates triggered a securities scam diverting funds to the tune of Rs 4000 crore (Rs 40 billion) from the banks to stockbrokers between April 1991 to May 1992. Harshad Mehta worked with the New India Assurance Company before he moved ahead to work in the stock markets. Mehta soon mastered the tricks of the trade and set out on dangerous game plan. Mehta has siphoned off huge sums of money from several banks and millions of investors were conned in the process. His scam was exposed, the markets crashed and he was arrested and banned for life from trading in the stock markets.

He was later charged with 72 criminal offences. A Special Court also sentenced Sudhir Mehta, Harshad Mehta's brother, and six others, including four bank officials, to rigorous imprisonment (RI) ranging from 1 year to 10 years on the charge of duping State Bank of India to the tune of Rs 600 crore (Rs 6 billion) in connection with the securities scam that rocked the financial markets in 1992. He died in 2002 with many litigations still pending against him.

(c) Ketan Parekh Scam

Ketan Parekh followed Harshad Mehta's footsteps to swindle crores of rupees from banks. A chartered accountant he used to run a family business, NH Securities. Ketan however had bigger plans in mind. He targetted smaller exchanges like the Allahabad Stock Exchange and the Calcutta Stock Exchange, and bought shares in fictitious names. His dealings revolved around shares of ten companies like Himachal Futuristic, Global Tele-Systems, SSI Ltd, DSQ Software, Zee Telefilms, Silverline, Pentamedia Graphics and Satyam Computer (K-10 scrips). Ketan borrowed Rs 250 crore from Global Trust Bank to fuel his ambitions. Ketan alongwith his associates also managed to get Rs 1,000 crore from the Madhavpura Mercantile Co-operative Bank.

According to RBI regulations, a broker was allowed a loan of only Rs 15 crore (Rs 150 million). There was evidence of price rigging in the scrips of Global Trust Bank, Zee Telefilms, HFCL, Lupin Laboratories, Aftek Infosys and Padmini Polymer.

(d) C R Bhansali Scam

The Bhansali scam resulted in a loss of over Rs 1,200 crore (Rs 12 billion). He first launched the finance company CRB Capital Markets, followed by CRB Mutual Fund and CRB Share Custodial Services. He ruled like a financial wizard 1992 to 1996 collecting money from the public through fixed deposits, bonds and debentures. The money was transferred to companies that never existed.

CRB Capital Markets raised a whopping Rs 176 crore in three years. In 1994 CRB Mutual Funds raised Rs 230 crore and Rs 180 crore came via fixed deposits. Bhansali also succeeded to raise about Rs 900 crore from the markets.

However, his good days did not last long, after 1995 he received several jolts. Bhansali tried borrowing more money from the market. This led to a financial crisis. It became difficult for Bhansali to sustain himself. The Reserve Bank of India (RBI) refused banking status to CRB and he was in the dock. SBI was one of the banks to be hit by his huge defaults. There was a need to assess what had been the response of the government, and what needed to be done to ensure that such scams did not recur in the future. The response of any government to a scam of the kind that occurred in India would have had three main facets:

1. Discover and Punish the Guilty

This task was entrusted to the Central Bureau of Investigation (CBI) and to the Joint Parliamentary Committee (JPC). A special court was also been set up to facilitate speedy trial.

2. Recover the Money

The draconian provisions of the Ordinance for attachment of property and voiding of transactions with the consequent creation of "tainted" shares were attempts in this direction.

3. Reform the System

The government's response so far has consisted of measures like banning of Ready Forward (RF) deals and going slow on liberalization. The Securities and Exchange Board of India (SEBI), in its capacity as overseer of the Indian Capital Market has witnessed eleven major scams. The Harshad Mehta scam of the early 1990s and the Ketan Parekh scam of the early 2000s are biggest. These scams were generated in the banking environment and they affected the investing community. When it happens, it degenerates into a dangerous force creating havoc in both the Money and Capital Markets. The scams bring lawlessness in the investment environment. The key perpetrators of the scam are the Stock Market intermediaries. The Securities and Exchange Board of India (SEBI), was formed in 1992 by the Government of India to oversee and regulate the Capital Market in the view of checking and stamping out the lawlessness that was growing and rendering the Capital Market unstable.

The Securities and Exchange Board of India (SEBI) is a Board (an autonomous body) created by the Government of India in 1988 and given statutory form in 1992 with the SEBI Act 1992. Its head office is in Mumbai, and other offices in Chennai, Kolkatta and Delhi. SEBI is the regulator of the Capital Markets in India. It is chaired by Mr. C.B. Bhave. The Board comprises of whole time members and outside members (representing the Finance Ministry, the Reserve Bank of India (RBI) and experts).

The term "securities scam" was defined as a skillful diversion of funds to the tune of over Rs. 3500 crores from the banking system to various stockbrokers in a series of transactions (primarily in Government securities). This plot took place during the period April 1991 to May 1992. In April 1992, the first press report appeared indicating that there was a shortfall in Government Securities held by the State Bank of India. In a little over a month, investigations revealed that the shortfall was just the tip of an iceberg which came to be called the securities scam. It involved the misappropriation of funds to the tune of over Rs. 3500 crores (about $ 1.2 billion). In an ever expanding ambit, the scam had engulfed top executives of large nationalized banks, foreign banks and financial institutions, brokers, bureaucrats and politicians. The functioning of the money market and the stock market had been thrown into disarray. The scam had generated such immense public interest that it had become a permanent feature on the front pages of national newspapers. A large number of agencies, namely, the Reserve Bank of India (RBI), the Central Bureau of Investigation (CBI), the Income Tax Department, the Directorate of Enforcement and the Joint Parliamentary Committee (JPC) all set out to investigate the various aspects of the scam, Barua and Varma (1993).

It was reported that the government responded to the scam with the promulgation of an ordinance and setting up of a special court to try those accused in the scam. The ordinance ordered attachment of property of all the accused and voided all transactions done by the accused brokers and their firms after April 1, 1991. These extraordinary measures were so harsh that even the purchases made by genuine investors were invalidated. All the shares that had been routed through the accused brokers were suspended from trading in the Capital Market, Barua and Varma (1993). This led to the creation of what came to be known as "tainted" shares. The tainted shares were worthless in the market as they could not be sold. This created a panic among investors and brokers and led to a prolonged closure of the Stock Exchanges along with a precipitous drop in the price of shares. In less than 2 months following the discovery of the scam, the stock prices dropped by over 40%, wiping out market value to the tune of Rs. 100,000 crores. The scam brought about a total "systems failure" which disrupted the Indian Capital Market.

The Impact of the Scam

The immediate impact of the scam was a sharp fall in the share prices. The index fell from 4500 to 2500, representing a loss of Rs. 100,000 crores in market capitalization. Besides the scam, there were other two major reasons for the fall: the first was the phenomenon of tainted shares which created panic in the market and second was the perceived slowdown of the reform process which destroyed the very foundation on which the boom was based. The government set up a special court and promulgated an ordinance with several draconian provisions to deal with the scam. Sections (3) and (4) of the ordinance attached the properties of all individuals accused in the scam and also voided all transactions that had at any stage been routed through them after March 31, 1991. Since the accused were Active brokers in the stock markets, the number of shares which had passed through their hands in the last one year was colossal. All these shares became "tainted" shares, and overnight they became worthless pieces of paper as they could not be delivered in the market. Genuine investors who had bought these shares well before the scam came to light and even got them registered in their names found themselves being robbed by the government. This resulted in a chaotic situation in the market, since no one was certain as to which shares were tainted and which were not.

The government's liberalization policies came under severe criticism after the scam, with Harshad Mehta and others being described as the products of these policies. Bowing to the political pressures and the bad press it received during the scam, the liberalization policies were put on hold for a while by the government. The Securities Exchange Board of India (SEBI) postponed sanctioning of private sector mutual funds. Implementation of some aspects of the Narasimham Committee recommendations on the banking system, were also delayed. Some question marks arose regarding privatization as the chairman of the committee looking into this ended up in jail on charges of involvement in the scam.

The much talked about entry of foreign pension funds and mutual funds became more remote than ever. The Euro-issues planned by several Indian companies were delayed, since the ability of Indian companies to raise equity capital in world markets was severely compromised.

The Harshad Mehta induced security scam, adversely affected at least 10 major commercial banks of India, a number of foreign banks operating in India, and the National Housing Bank, a subsidiary of the Reserve Bank of India, which is the central bank of India.

As an aftermath of the shockwaves which engulfed the Indian financial sector, a number of people holding key positions in the India's financial sector were adversely affected. However, some people were disciplined, amidst these things included the arrest and sacking of K. M. Margabandhu, the then CMD of the UCO Bank; the removal from office of V. Mahadevan, one of the Managing Directors of India's largest bank.

Policy Responses Required

It is clear that the government, the RBI and the commercial banks are as much accountable as the brokers for the scam. The brokers were encouraged and abetted by the banks to divert funds from the banking system to the stock market. The RBI too stands indicted because despite knowledge about banks over-stepping the boundaries demarcating their arena of operations, it failed to reign them in. The looting was done with active connivance and sometimes full knowledge of the very individuals who were supposed to guard against such a possibility. What has been the response of the government so far and what needs to be done to ensure that such scams do not recur in the future?

The response of any government to a scam of this kind would have three main facets:

1. **Discover and punish the guilty** - this task was entrusted to the Central Bureau of Investigation (CBI) and to the Joint Parliamentary Committee (JPC) for execution. A special court was also set up to facilitate speedy trial of the accused.
2. **Recover the money** - the draconian provisions of the Ordinance for attachment of property and voiding of all transactions with the consequent creation of "tainted" shares were attempts in this direction.

3. **Reform the system** - the government's response, consisted of measures like banning of RF deals and going slow on liberalization. The market watchdog, Securities and Exchange Board of India, banned Harshad Mehta for life from stock market-related Activities. There cannot be two opinions on the need for identifying and punishing the guilty. The principal objective behind punishing the offenders was more to deter future offenders and restore the confidence of the investors.

However, the government ensured that not only the obviously guilty (the brokers), but also the not so obviously guilty (the bank executives, the bureaucrats and perhaps the politicians) were identified and brought to book.

Investigations of this kind are necessarily time consuming and expensive, but they have to be gone through, so that the credibility of the system be restored. A rule of thumb which is often quoted throughout the world is that investigation of any fraud may cost as much as the magnitude of the fraud itself. One can, therefore, expect the real costs of the scam investigation to be of the order of a couple of thousand crores at least.

While recovery of the money swindled from the banks was important, the method employed by the government to do that was extremely ham handed and unfair. However, the government had to implore special powers to recover the siphoned money to enable the system back to normal. It was an attempt to redress the system failure situation. There was justification for such measures as the "tainted" shares law, though it harassed genuine innocent investors.

The most constructive response to the scam was in the arena of reforms of the financial system. This is because the origins of the scam resulted from the over-regulation of the markets.

The regulations in the money markets were such that thoroughly legitimate and essential transactions could not be put through openly, but had to be disguised and camouflaged.

Lessons from the Scam Activities

The role of the brokers and of some of the banks as market makers was not recognized and they could perform these important and useful functions only by subterfuge. The payment and clearance system was so antiquated and cumbersome that totally indefensible methods had to be adopted to achieve speedy funds transfers. The net result of all these was a total lack of transparency in the operations in the money market. Irregularities of all kinds were so common that no suspicions were aroused even by highly irregular transactions. The situation was an ideal environment for a scam to germinate and grow to alarming proportions. Some of the control systems in the banks broke down, because they had been deliberately allowed to be weakened by both the commercial banks as well as the RBI in order to facilitate normal transactions in violation of the RBI guidelines.

The other lesson from the scam is that artificial insulation of closely related markets from each other is counterproductive in the long run. Just as water finds its own level, money also seeks out the highest levels of return after due adjustments for risk and liquidity. Even after twenty years of progressive liberalization of the Indian financial markets, artificial barriers still exist between the money market and the stock market, between the market for corporate securities and the market for government securities and between the formal money market and the informal one. It is necessary to allow for the integration of these markets to encourage the smooth flow of transactions and growth. This integration will allow a coherent yield curve to emerge covering the entire financial markets. The recommendations of the Nadkarni Committee set up in the wake of the scam, to examine the functioning of the money market, that RF deals were permitted and that the entire settlement and clearing system be carefully streamlined and computerized, and taken seriously by the various operators.

The Strategy of the Scam

The crucial mechanism through which the scam was perpetrated was the **Ready Forward** (RF) deal. The RF is in essence a secured short term (typically 15 day) loan from one bank to another bank. The lending is done against government securities, exactly the way a pawn broker lends against jewellery or other valuables. A ready forward deal is, in substance, a secured loan from one bank to another. To make the scam possible, the RF deal had to undergo a complete metamorphosis: it had to become **an unsecured loan to a broker**. The three crucial steps to the accomplishment of the metamorphosis were:

i. **The settlement process** - the settlement process in the government Securities Market became broker intermediated, that is, delivery and payments started getting routed through a broker instead of being made directly between the transacting banks.

ii. **The broker** - the broker through whom the payment passed on its way from one bank to another found a way of crediting the money into his account though the account payee cheque was drawn in favour of a bank. This was done by way of negotiation on interest basis.

iii. **Security for the loan** - while the above two steps transformed an RF deal from a loan to a bank into a loan to a broker, it would still be a secured loan. However, the brokers soon found a way of persuading the lending bank to dispense with security for the loan or to accept worthless security. This was in contravention of banking rules and regulations, which yielded to the modus operandi used by the scam.

The modus operandi used in the scam, however, in form, was the Ready Forward (RF) deal, which was not a loan at all. The borrowing bank (Bank 2) actually sold the securities to the lending bank (Bank 1) and bought them back at the end of the period of the deal at (typically) a slightly higher price. The price difference represented the profit on the deal. The RF is what in other countries is known as a repurchase (or repo) agreement. It is a very safe and secure form of lending and is very common throughout the world. The US Repo Market, for example, is about a hundred times larger than the Indian RF market. However, in the Indian Capital Market, the brokers managed and got hold of the system and engineered it for their benefit.

The RF in India Serves Two Main Purposes

Like repo markets around the world the RF deals provide much needed liquidity to the government Securities Markets.

The RF deals are an important tool in the hands of the banks to manage their Statutory Liquidity Ratio (SLR) requirements. Banks in India were required to maintain 38.5% of their demand and time liabilities (DTL) in government securities and certain approved securities which are collectively known as SLR securities. RF helps in managing this requirement in two ways: a). A bank which has a temporary surge in DTL may not want to buy SLR securities outright and then sell them when the DTL comes back to normal. Instead it can do an RF deal, whereby it effectively borrows the securities from a bank which has surplus SLR securities. An RF in SLR securities can thus be seen either as lending of money or as borrowing of securities. b). An RF deal is not legally a loan. The amount borrowed by a bank under RF is not regarded as a part of the bank's liabilities. Therefore it is not a part of its DTL, and does not attract the SLR requirement. Had the bank borrowed outright, it would have had to maintain 38.5% of the borrowing in SLR securities.

Settlement Process

The normal settlement process in government securities is that the transacting banks make payments and deliver the securities directly to each other. The broker's only function is to bring the buyer and seller together and help them negotiate the terms, for which he earns a commission from both the parties. The broker does not handle either the cash or the securities. During the scam, however, the banks or at least some banks adopted an alternative settlement process which was similar to the process used for settling transactions in the stock market. In this settlement process, deliveries of securities and payments are made through the broker. That is, the seller hands over the securities to the broker who passes them on to the buyer, while the buyer gives the cheque to the broker who then makes the payment to the seller. In this settlement process, the buyer and the seller may not even know whom they have traded with, both being known only to the broker.

There were two important reasons why the brokers' intermediated settlement system began to be used in the government Securities Markets:

1. The brokers instead of merely bringing buyers and sellers together started taking positions in the market. In other words, they started trading on their own account, and in a sense became market makers in some securities thereby imparting greater liquidity to the markets.
2. When a bank wanted to conceal the fact that it was doing an RF deal, the broker came in handy. The broker provided contract notes for this purpose with fictitious counterparties, but arranged for the Actual settlement to take place with the correct counterparty. A broker intermediated settlement allowed the broker to lay his hands on the cheque as it went from one bank to another through him. The hurdle now was to find a way of crediting the cheque to his account though it was drawn in favour of a bank and was crossed account payee.

As it happens, it is purely a matter of banking custom that an account payee cheque is paid only to the payee mentioned on the cheque. In fact, exceptions were being made to this norm, well before the scam came to light. Privileged (corporate) customers were routinely allowed to credit account payee cheques in favour of a bank into their own accounts to avoid clearing delays, thereby reducing the interest lost on the amount.

Normally, if a customer obtains a cheque in his own favour and deposits it into his own account, it may take a day or two for the cheque to be cleared and for the funds to become available to the customer. At 15% interest, the interest loss on a clearing delay of two days for a Rs. 100 crore cheque is about Rs. 8 lacs. On the other hand, when banks make payments to each other by writing cheques on their account with the RBI, these cheques are cleared on the same day. The practice which thus emerged was that a customer would obtain a cheque drawn on the RBI favouring not himself but his bank.

The bank would get the money and credit his account the same day. This was the practice which the brokers in the money market used and exploited the market to their benefit. The brokers thus found a way of getting hold of the cheques as they went from one bank to another and crediting the amounts to their accounts. This effectively transformed an RF into a loan to a broker rather than to a bank. But this, by itself, would not have led to the scam, because the RF after all is a secured loan, and a secured loan to a broker is still secured. What was necessary now was to find a way of eliminating the security itself. Some banks (or rather their officials) were persuaded to part with cheques without actually receiving securities in return. A simple explanation of this is that the officials concerned were bribed and/or negligent. A more intriguing possibility is that the banks' senior/top management were aware of this and turned a Nelson's eye to it, largely because of the benefit of the higher returns the brokers could offer by diverting the funds to the stock market. One must recognize that as long as the scam lasted, the banks benefited from such an arrangement. The management of banks might have been sorely tempted to adopt this route to higher profitability.

The second route was to replace the Actual securities by a worthless piece of paper – a fake Bank Receipt (BR). This is discussed in greater detail in the next section.

The third method was simply to forge the securities themselves. In many cases, PSU bonds were represented only by allotment letters rather than certificates on security paper. And it is easier to forge an allotment letter for Rs. 100 crores worth of securities than it is to forge a 100 rupee note! Outright forgery of this kind however accounted for only a very small part of the total funds misappropriated.

Bank Receipt

In an RF deal, the borrowing bank delivers the Actual securities to the lender and takes them back on repayment of the loan. In practice, however, this is not usually done. Instead, the borrower gives a Bank Receipt (BR) which serves three functions:

The BR confirms the sale of securities. It Acts as a receipt for the money received by the selling bank, hence, Bank Receipt. It promised to deliver the securities to the buyer. It also stated that in the meantime the seller held the securities in trust for the buyer.

In short, a BR was something like an IOU (I owe you securities!), and the use of the BR de facto converted an RF deal into an unsecured loan. The lending bank no longer had the securities; it had only the borrower's assurance that the borrower had the securities which could/were delivered if/when the need arose. There were several reasons why BRs came to be used in lieu of the actual securities:

BRs were very convenient for RF deals because delivery was not needed. BRs could simply be cancelled and returned when the deals were reversed In case of PSU bonds, actual delivery was almost impossible because of a variety of reasons, such as non-existence of certificates, or a single certificate for investment of several hundreds of crores of rupees. In case of government securities, the RBI had issued a directive that BRs should not be used. The reason was that, for these securities, the RBI, through its Public Debt Office (PDO), Acts as the custodian. Physical securities are never issued, and the holding of these securities is represented by book entries at the PDO. The ledger in which the PDO maintains these accounts is called the Subsidiary General Ledger (SGL), and these securities are referred to as SGL securities. When the holder of these securities sold them and wished to transfer them to the buyer, he filled up an SGL transfer form and gave it to the buyer. This SGL form could be compared to a cheque: the buyer deposits it into his SGL account at the PDO, and the PDO made a book entry reducing the holding of the seller and increasing that of the buyer. Because of this facility, the RBI did not permit use of BRs for these securities. Had the PDO functioned efficiently and carried out its bookkeeping without delays, RBI would have been justified in not permitting the use of BRs for government securities. Unfortunately, the PDO was very inefficient and laggardly in its functioning. This was a very serious matter, because, like a cheque, an SGL form can also bounce, if the seller does not have sufficient holding of securities in his SGL account. The buyer needs to be informed about this promptly; else, he may resell the same securities by issuing his own SGL forms in the belief that he has sufficient balance in his account. The inefficiency of the PDO made the SGL form an inconvenient and unreliable instrument, and banks preferred to use BRs even for the SGL securities, in violation of the RBI's directive. As stated earlier, a BR was supposed to imply that the issuer actually got the securities and holds them in trust for the buyer. But in reality the issuer never got the securities at all.

There are two reasons why a bank issued a BR which was not backed by actual securities:

A bank may short sell securities, that is, it sells securities it does not have. This would be done if the bank thinks that the prices of these securities would decrease. Since this would be an outright sale (not an RF), the bank issues a BR. When the securities did fall in value, the bank bought them at lower prices and discharges the BR by delivering the securities sold. Short selling in some form was an integral part of most bond markets. It could be argued that some amount of short selling subject to some degree of regulation was a desirable feature of a bond market. An outright sale using a BR which was not backed by securities was not harmful per se though it violates the RBI guidelines. The second reason was that the bank may simply wanted an unsecured loan. It then carried out an RF deal issuing a "fake" BR which is a BR without any securities to back them. The lending bank would be under a mistaken impression that it is making a secured loan when it is actually advancing an unsecured loan. Obviously, lenders should have taken measures to protect themselves from such a possibility.

During the scam, the brokers perfected the art of using fake BRs to obtain unsecured loans from the banking system. They persuaded some small and little known banks – the Bank of Karad (BOK) and the Metropolitan Cooperative Bank (MCB) - to issue BRs as and when required. These BRs could then be used to do RF deals with other banks. The cheques in favour of BOK were, of course, credited into the brokers' accounts. In effect, several large banks made huge unsecured loans to the BOK/MCB which in turn made the money available to the brokers.

Control Systems

The scam was made possible by a complete breakdown of the control system both within the commercial banks as well as the control system of the RBI itself. We shall examine these control systems to understand how these failed to function effectively and what lessons can be learnt to prevent failure of control systems in the future.

The internal control system of the commercial banks involves the following features:

(i) Separation of Functions

The different aspects of securities transactions of a bank, namely dealing, custody and accounting are carried out by different persons. Dealing refers to the decision about which transactions are to be entered into with which parties. Custody involves receiving and delivering securities/substitute instruments and cheques for the transactions done. Accounting involves maintenance of the investment account of the bank and its reconciliation with the SGL account of the bank maintained by the PDO of the RBI.

Closely related to separation of functions is the notion of double custody. Just as the currency chests in the banks are under double custody where two people have to collaborate to open it, the securities too are usually under double custody. The assumption underlying double custody is that two individuals are unlikely to have a criminal intent at the same time. In many banks like the National Housing Bank, these controls did not exist. In others, such as the State Bank of India, they existed but broke down partially or wholly because of the negligence of one or more of the functionaries.

(ii) Counterparty Limits

The moment an RF deal is done on the basis of a BR rather than Actual securities, the lending bank has to contend with the possibility that the BR received may not be backed by any/adequate securities. In effect, therefore, it may be making an unsecured loan, and it must do the RF only if it is prepared to make an unsecured loan. This requires assessing the creditworthiness of the borrower and assigning him a "credit limit" up to which the bank is prepared to lend. Technically, this is known as a counterparty limit. Strictly, a counterparty limit is required even if an RF is done against Actual securities because the securities may decline in value and the RF may end up becoming only partly secured though it was fully secured to begin with. Most of the foreign banks with the exception of the Standard Chartered Bank had very strict counterparty limits and were thus protected from lending too much against fake BRs. For a bank like the Bank of Karad, a reasonable counterparty limit may have been Rs. 50 *lakhs* so that an RF for several hundred crores would be flatly refused. The Standard Chartered Bank either did not have or did not adhere to such limits and agreed to do these RFs.

(iii) Control System of the RBI should Ideally Involve the following

The PDO keeps track of the aggregate of each type of government security claimed by all the banks and ensures that the figures tally with the aggregate value of the securities at the end of each day. If all BRs are backed by securities, the seller's investment account would decrease and the buyer's account would increase by the transaction amount, leaving the aggregate unchanged.

A reconciliation of the SGL securities claimed by each bank through mandatory periodic statements with the total holding as recorded in the SGL account (of the bank) at the PDO, would help in pin-pointing the banks whose accounts need to be investigated.

These simple control mechanisms were not being operated by the PDO. What is more surprising is that even when discrepancies were discovered, such as when some SGL forms sent to the PDO bounced because of inadequate inventory of securities in the seller's account, the intimation regarding the inadequacy of securities was communicated to the buyer leisurely, may be through a letter by ordinary post, which could take days to reach. In the meantime, if the buyer sells the same securities on the strength of the SGL sent to the PDO, it could start an ever expanding chain of bounced SGLs. It appears that the PDO was not particularly perturbed by such possibilities.

The RBI is expected to carry out site inspections and other audits of the investment accounts and procedures of the banks. These were not quite comprehensive and even when some irregularities were detected, the RBI did not Act decisively against the erring banks.

Coupon Changes and Insider Trading

During the period from September 1991 to June 1992, the government raised the interest (coupon) rate on its fresh borrowing three times. On each occasion the coupon rate was increased by 1/2%, thereby raising the coupon rate from 11.5% to 13% during this ten month period. The major implication of raising interest rate on new borrowings is that it would trigger a fall in the market prices of the old loans which are pegged at the old (lower) interest rates. The price of the 11.5% Government Loan 2010 dropped by 3% to 5% with each coupon rate hike.

If anyone has advance information about these changes in the coupon rates, he could make enormous amounts of riskless profit by short selling the old securities just before the announcement of rate hike and buying back (covering his position) after the prices have fallen. Somebody who took a short position of Rs. 500 crores before the coupon hike of September 1991 could have made a profit of Rs. 15 crores, practically overnight! Since several persons in the Finance Ministry and the RBI are likely to be aware of the impending hike in the coupon rate, the chance of leakage of this all important information is always there. There have been several allegations in this regard. However, it was probably very difficult to prove with any degree of certainty that there was insider trading based on information about coupon rate changes, because of the size of the market. With a daily trading volume of Rs. 3000 - 4000 crore, it was very easy for anyone to take a position (based on inside information) of Rs. 500 or even Rs. 1000 crore without anyone suspecting anything untoward.

Most banks carried investments in their books at their cost of acquisition and did not mark them down to market. This created serious distortions during a period when, the prices of securities were falling. If one assumed that the prices of government securities fell by about 5% over the last year, then on an aggregate holding of these securities by the banking system of Rs. 70,000 crores, the paper loss of the banks was going to be Rs. 3,500 crores. A 10% fall in the prices of PSU bonds implied a further paper loss of about Rs. 800 crores to the banks (based on the assessment that banks held about Rs. 8000 crores worth of PSU bonds). Under the current system of accounting, such losses are recognized only when the securities are sold. This meant that, a bank could be reluctant to sell the securities and show the loss in its books. It was in this context that the banks and the brokers resorted to innovative methods of window dressing the banks' balance sheets. The basic idea was as follows:

a. The bank sold the securities trading at a discount to a broker at face value or at a price which was much higher than the prevailing market prices. The broker incurred a huge loss in this transaction as he in turn resold the securities to some other bank at market prices.

b. The bank then buys some other securities from the same broker at prices well above market prices. The broker therefore makes a huge profit in the second transaction which compensates him for the loss incurred in transaction (a). Thus, the net result of the two transactions is that neither the bank nor the broker makes any profit or loss. Then why would these transactions done? The reason is that while the profit earned through transaction (a) would improve the bottom line (profit) for the bank, the loss suffered by the bank in transaction (b) would not be reflected in its profit and loss account at all. The securities bought would simply appear in the bank's balance sheet at inflated values! It is a most ingenious way of creating paper profits. As far the broker is concerned, the price in transaction (a) can be as high as the bank wants so long as he gets a correspondingly higher price in transaction (b). What the scam investigations revealed was that window dressing of this kind was rampant. Instances were recorded of the same broker selling the same security on the same day to different banks at vastly different prices. This made it very difficult to fathom the motives for a single transaction in isolation from other transactions done by a bank. It demanded that one put together the entire series of transactions; otherwise, it was impossible to know whether the banks or the brokers had been the net gainers through all the manipulative transactions. It was conceivable that some brokers were willing to absorb a part of the losses as a quid pro quo for other "services" which the banks provided them. It was interesting to note that even the pure RF deal involved an element of window dressing. The lending bank showed the interest received as an income in its profit and loss account. The borrowing bank did not show the interest paid as an expense, because it simply carried the investment in its books at the higher repurchase price. It was, in fact, quite likely that the enormous increases in the profits that some of the banks reported in 1992 over the previous year, could at least in part be explained by the use of such "creative" accounting practices.

Where has All the Money Gone?

It was becoming increasingly clear that despite the intensive efforts by several investigating agencies, it was impossible to trace all the money swindled from the banks. Based on the result of investigations and reporting, the following were the possibilities:

A large amount of the money was perhaps invested in shares. However, since the share prices had dropped steeply from the peak they reached towards end of March 1992, the important question was what were the shares worth then? Till February 1992, the Bombay Sensitive Index was below 2000; thereafter, it rose sharply to peak at 4500 by end of March 1992. In the aftermath of the scam it fell to about 2500 before recovering to around 3000 by August 1992. Going by newspaper reports, it was that the bulk of Harshad Mehta's purchases were made at low prices, so that the average cost of his portfolio corresponded to an index well below 2500 or perhaps even below 2000. It was well known in the Indian Capital Market, that while Harshad Mehta was the "big bull" in the Stock Market, there was an equally powerful "bear cartel", represented by Hiten Dalal, A.D. Narottam and others, who operated in the market with money dupe out of the banking system. Since the stock prices rose steeply during the period of the scam, it was found out that a considerable part of the money swindled by this group had been spent on financing the losses in the stock markets. Part of the money was sent out of India through the Havala Racket, converted into dollars/pounds, and brought back as India Development Bonds. These bonds were redeemable in dollars/pounds and the holders cannot be asked to disclose the source of their holdings. Thus, this money was beyond the reach of any of the investigating agencies. A part of the money must have been spent as bribes and kickbacks to the various accomplices in the banks and in the bureaucracy and in the political system. In all there are reforms of both the primary and secondary capital markets.

Table 5.2: Major Reforms in the Primary Market

S.N	Type of Reform
1	Merit-based regime to disclosure-based regime. Disclosure and Investor Protection. **Guidelines issued**.
2	Pricing of public issues determined by the market.
3	System of proportional allotment of shares introduced.
4	Banks and public sector undertakings allowed to raise funds from the primary market.
5	Accounting standards close to international standards
6	Corporate Governance Guidelines issued.
7	Discretionary allotment system to QIBs has been withdrawn
8	Mutual funds are encouraged in both the public and private sectors and have been given permission to invest overseas and Guidelines were issued for private placement of debt.
9	Securities and Exchange Board of India promotes Self-Regulatory Organizations.
10	Allocation to retail investors increased from 25 percent to 35 percent.
11	Separate allocation of 5 percent to domestic mutual funds within the QIB category.
12	Freedom to fix face value of shares below Rs. 10 per share only in cases where the issue price is Rs. 50 or more.
13	Shares allotted on a preferential basis as well as the pre-allotment holding are subjected to lock-in period of six months to prevent sale of shares.

Source: Securities and Exchange Board of India (SEBI)

Table 5.3: Major Reforms in the Secondary Market

S.N	Type of Reform
1	Registration of market intermediaries made mandatory.
2	Capital adequacy norms specified for brokers and sub-brokers of Stock Exchanges.
3	Guidelines issued on Listing Agreement between Stock Exchanges and corporates.
4	Settlement cycle shortened to T+2.
5	Stock Exchanges and other intermediaries, including mutual funds, inspected.
6	Regulation of Substantial Acquisition of Shares and Takeovers, 1997.
7	Foreign institutional investors (FIIs) allowed to invest in Indian Capital Market, 1992.
8	Order-driven, fully automatic, anonymous screen-based trading introduced.
9	Depositories Act, 1996, enacted.
10	Guidelines issued on Corporate Governance.
11	Fraudulent and unfair trade practices, including insider trading, prohibited by Securities and Exchange Board of India.
12	Straight-through processing introduced and made mandatory for institutional trades.
13	Margin trading and securities lending and borrowing schemes introduced.
14	Separate trading platform, Indonext, for small and medium-sized enterprises (SME) sector launched.
15	Notification of corporatization and demutualization of Stock Exchanges.
16	Settlement and trade guarantee fund and investor protection fund set up.
17	Comprehensive risk management system (capital adequacy, trading and exposure limit, margin requirement, index-based market-wide circuit breaker, online position monitoring, automatic disablement of terminals) put in place.
18	Comprehensive surveillance system put in place.
19	Securities Appellate Tribunal set up July 28, 1997.
20	Mutual funds and FIIs to begin entering the unique client code (UCC) pertaining to the parent entity at the order-entry level and entered UCCs for individual schemes and sub-accounts for the post-closing session.
21	Introduction of exchange traded derivatives in India in June 2000.

Source: Securities and Exchange Board of India (SEBI)

Table 5.4: Securities Regulations and Guidelines in Effect

S.N	Type of Regulations and Guidelines
1	SEBI (Stockbrokers and Sub-Brokers) Regulations, 1992
2	SEBI (Prohibition of Insider Trading) Regulations, 1992
3	SEBI (Merchant Bankers) Regulations, 1992
4	SEBI (Portfolio Managers) Regulations, 1993
5	SEBI (Registrars to an Issue and Share Transfer Agents) Regulations, 1993
6	SEBI (Underwriters) Regulations, 1993
7	SEBI (Debenture Trustees) Regulations, 1993
8	SEBI (Bankers to an Issue) Regulations, 1994
9	SEBI (Foreign Institutional Investors) Regulations, 1995
10	SEBI (Custodian of Securities) Regulations, 1996

11	SEBI (Depositories and Participants) Regulations, 1996
12	SEBI (Venture Capital Funds) Regulations, 1996
13	SEBI (Mutual Funds) Regulations, 1996
14	SEBI (Substantial Acquisition of Shares and Takeovers) Regulations, 1997
15	SEBI (Buyback of Securities) Regulations, 1998
16	SEBI (Credit Rating Agencies) Regulations, 1999
17	SEBI (Collective Investment Schemes) Regulations, 1999
18	SEBI (Foreign Venture Capital Investors) Regulations, 2000
19	SEBI (Procedure for Board Meeting) Regulations, 2001
20	SEBI (Issue of Sweat Equity) Regulations, 2002
21	SEBI (Procedure for Holding Inquiry by Inquiry Officer and Imposing Penalty)
22	**Regulations, 2002** SEBI (Prohibition of Fraudulent and Unfair Trade Practices Relating to Securities Markets)
	Regulations, 2003
23	SEBI (Central Listing Authority) Regulations, 2003
24	SEBI (Ombudsman) Regulations, 2003
25	SEBI (Central Database of Market Participants) Regulations, 2003
26	SEBI (Self-Regulatory Organizations) Regulations, 2004
27	SEBI (Criteria for Fit and Proper Person) Regulations, 2004
28	Securities Contracts (Regulation) (Manner of Increasing and Maintaining Public Shareholding in Recognized Stock Exchanges) Regulations, 2006
29	SEBI (Regulatory Fee On Stock Exchanges) Regulations, 2006
30	SEBI (Certification Of Associated Persons In The Securities Markets) Regulations, 2007
31	Notification under Securities and Exchange Board of India (Certification of Associated Persons in the Securities Markets) Regulations, 2007
32	SEBI (Public Offer and Listing of Securitised Debt Instruments) Regulations, 2008
33	SEBI (Intermediaries) Regulations, 2008
34	SEBI (Issue and Listing of Debt Securities) Regulations, 2008
35	Securities and Exchange Board of India (Investor Protection and Education Fund) Regulations, 2009
	Guidelines
36	SEBI (Employee Stock Option Scheme and Employee Stock Purchase Scheme)
	Guidelines,1999
37	Guidelines for Opening of Trading Terminals Abroad (Issued in 1999)
38	SEBI (Disclosure and Investor Protection) Guidelines, 2000
39	SEBI (Delisting of Securities) Guidelines, 2003
40	SEBI (STP Centralized Hub and STP Service Providers) Guidelines, 2004
41	Comprehensive Guidelines for Investor Protection Fund/Customer Protection Fund at Stock Exchanges (Issued in 2004)
	Schemes
42	Securities Lending Scheme, 1997
43	SEBI (Informal Guidance) Scheme, 2003

Source: Securities and Exchange Board of India.

The Capital Market Regulator, SEBI has carefully developed good stability mechanisms to keep the Market functioning in a sustainable manner. There are difficulties, but the Capital Market Regulator devises careful working strategies to overcome them. Such strategies come in the form of rules, regulations and innovative market reforms. SEBI has been granted powers by the Law Courts and the Government of India which help it machinery to function as expected. SEBI is very much engaged in the education of investors and the careful training of all Capital Market participants. This is the source of stability and sustainability in the Indian Capital Market. The situation of the Indian Capital Market is evidence of the fact investors' interest is well protected. They should have confidence in the market and invest without fear of or abnormal excess losses.

Why Bring in Capital Market Reforms

The Securities Market in India was underdeveloped, opaque, dominated by a handful of players, and concentrated in a few cities. Manipulation and unfair practices were perceived to be rampant, prompting an overseas researcher to describe the market as a "snake pit." The transformation of the Indian Securities Market started with the establishment of the Securities and Exchange Board of India (SEBI) in 1989, initially as an informal body and in 1992 as a statutory autonomous regulator with the twin objectives of protecting the interests of investors and developing and regulating the Securities Market over a period of time. SEBI has been empowered to investigate, examine, visit company premises, summon records and persons, and inquire and impose penalties commensurate with misconduct. The first and foremost challenge for SEBI was to create a regulatory and supervisory framework for the market, a job that proved formidable, because vested interests resisted every new step.

However, with the designing and notification of regulations and guidelines, the apparatus steadily evolved and the Capital Market has adapted to the situation.

SEBI has instituted a consultative process of framing regulations. All reports, concept papers, and policy proposals are posted on SEBI's website (www.sebi.gov.in) for comments from market participants and the public. The comments are compiled and taken into account before regulations are finalized. All draft regulations are put on the website, so that legal experts can comment on the law's correspondence with the spirit of the initiatives. This openness has a profound impact not only in terms of valuable input and gauging public opinion before framing regulations and guidelines but also in terms of improving quality, acceptability, and ease of implementation. SEBI has formed a number of committees of eminent experts and market practitioners to support it in the design of reforms for different aspects of Securities

Markets. The regulator posts all its orders, including those delivered on appeals against its orders, on its website. On request, it provides informal guidance on payments of nominal fees and issues an Action letter so that the participants can seek clarification on any aspect and adopt an appropriate business strategy that conforms to the applicable regulations.

SEBI has put timelines for performance of its various functions, such as registration and renewal, on the website. These measures work as a self-disciplining mechanism within SEBI and provide full transparency to its functioning.

Reforms in the Primary Market (Table 5.2)

The primary market, which at one time was flooded with a number of issues floated by dubious promoters, depriving gullible investors of their lifetime savings, has since been transformed. The changes in this area have been epic and include detailing of complete profiles of promoters; comprehensive disclosures, the existence of tangible assets, and a track record of profit as also reporting end uses of funds to the Board as a part of Corporate Governance. Recently, when the story of Google's initial public offering (IPO) was being touted in the media worldwide as one of the greatest innovations of recent times for raising risk capital, the Financial Times, London, carried the following observation: The World's Biggest Democracy can show Google how to conduct an online IPO. In India you cannot apply on the web but investors can access one of the world's largest financial networks with 7000 terminals scattered around 350 cities. And every step of the book building process is public... The Indian system is a refreshing example of a transparent IPO market but it is also a rare one, especially in the insider-friendly Asian markets.

All the IPOs, since the reforms started have been a success and barely a few exceptions are trading at a premium over the issue price. The regulatory framework has been modified to provide options to Indian firms for raising resources either domestically, globally, or both. These options help discover prices and reduce the cost of funds. A number of Indian firms have raised money through American depository receipts, global depository receipts, and external commercial borrowings. The two-way (internal and external) fundability was permitted to enhance liquidity.

During 2004–05, a sum of Rs. 282.56 billion, as opposed to Rs. 232.71 billion in 2003–04 (which was larger than the amount raised in the 10 years of the earlier primary market boom), was raised through the primary market. The corporate sector and central and state governments together raised a total of Rs. 3.75 trillion from the Securities Market during

2004–05. However, no major mishap has occurred recently, but how prepared is the Indian Capital Market for the 2011 Capital Market Scam?

The quality of the secondary market of India has been tremendously upgraded. The deafening noise of an outcry trading system has been replaced with the silence of the electronic consolidated anonymous limit order book, with price-time priority matching accessible through more than 10,000 terminals spread over 400 cities and towns across the Indian subcontinent. It is not an over evaluation to say that it is something perhaps without a parallel in the world. Transaction costs are lower, compared with those of the most developed markets.

The Indian Capital Market Settlement System

The Indian settlement system conforms to the Committee on Payment and Settlement–International Organization of Securities Commissions principles and G–30 committee (January 2003, under the chairmanship of Sir Andrew Large) recommendations, which even the most developed markets of the world are proposing to implement. The institution of the central counterparty (CCP), which provides full innovation and guarantees settlement, has eliminated counterparty risk entirely. More than 99 percent of the dematerialization of market capitalization and straight-through processing, mandatory for all institutional trades, had enabled the Indian settlement system to function seamlessly, notwithstanding size and spread.

On a T+2 cycle, all securities are fully cleared electronically through a CCP on a rolling settlement. The CCP of the exchanges, which operates a tight risk management system and maintains a short (T+2) and consistent settlement cycle, is now financially able to meet the obligations for four to five consecutive settlements even if all the trading members default in their obligations. The dynamic risk management system comprises capital adequacy norms, trading and exposure limits, index-based market-wide circuit breakers, and margin (mark to market) requirements.

The encashability of the underlying liquidity of the margins, comprising cash, bank guarantees, and securities, is evaluated periodically. The real-time monitoring of broker positions and margins and automatic disablement of terminals with value-added risk margining, built on much higher sigma deviation than the best of the markets in the world, have reduced the operational risk to the lowest ebb. In a recent unfortunate, very sharp (more than 25 percent in two days) fall of the market in May 2004, the strength of the system's risk management was tested. There was not a single broker failure or default, and on the third day (after the two consecutive days of decline) the market functioned as if nothing unusual had happened. Even the CCP was not required to fund any broker-dealer's obligations.

The State of the Indian Capital Market Today

The state of the market today bears testimony to the role SEBI plays. A study by the Society for Capital Market Research and Development (October 2004) revealed that there has been great improvement in the general public's perception of Capital Market regulation in India since 2001.

The Economic Survey 2003–04 by the government of India had the following to say: "The Securities Markets have made enormous progress in recent years. India's equity market is now being increasingly recognized as a success story on the world scale." These reforms have boosted the confidence of investors (domestic and international) in the Indian securities market. There are four parameters to ascertain the level of investor confidence: (1) investments by foreign institutional investors (FIIs), (2) growth of the mutual funds industry, (3) subscriptions to IPOs, and (4) an increase in the number of accounts with the depositories. The figures from the 2003–04 financial year, mutual funds mobilized net resources of about Rs. 480 billion, equivalent to about one-fourth of incremental bank deposits. Mutual funds' assets increased from Rs. 1.1 billion at the end of March 2003 to Rs. 2.0 billion at the end of October 2005. Indian companies raised about Rs. 33 billion through euro issues.

The year 2004 witnessed a net FII (portfolio money) inflow of US$10 billion. The volume of issuance in the primary market increased from Rs. 41 billion in 2002–03 to Rs. 282.56 billion in 2004–05. The two benchmark stock market indices, namely the SENSEX and S&P CNX NIFTY, generated astounding returns of 83 percent and 81 percent, respectively, during 2002–03 and 2003–04. Market capitalization grew from Rs. 7 trillion at the end of March 2003 to Rs. 14 trillion at the end of March 2004, and to Rs. 23 trillion as of August 2005, indicating that the equity market is bigger than the banking system. The primary issues in the last year added at least Rs. 2 trillion in market capitalization. The trading in cash segment of exchanges increased from Rs. 932,062 in 2002-03 to Rs. 1,658,787 in 2004–05. Trading in derivatives increased from Rs. 442,341 to Rs. 2,563,165 during the same period. The turnover in government securities increased from Rs. 1,941,621 to Rs. 2,639,897. The impact cost went down to 0.1 percent in 2003–04, reflecting substantial improvement in liquidity. The number of demand accounts with depository participants has increased considerably during the past three years, from 3.8 million to 8 million, and is increasing on average at the rate of more than 100,000 per month. The number of investor complaints received by SEBI has been sharply decreasing over the years. The efficacy of the market, where entry and exit are possible at will and the liquidity has spread from being skewed to just about 100 to more than 500 securities, is a matter of substantial comfort. More than 2,500 securities (equities) are traded for more than 100 days in a year. Overseas investors are no longer glued to research and assessments of index stocks and have been observing keenly and investing in the mid-cap segment. The changes in the market have been very fast-paced; they have been possible with the cooperation of all the market participants, other regulators, and the government of India. The impression is not that in the Indian Securities Market everything was fine and needed no improvement, polishing, or refurbishing. The dynamics of the global environment dictates that those charged with the responsibility of bringing about changes must always seek out learning by experience, criticism, and judgments. The market depth needs to be supplemented with further product diversification— mortgage- and asset-backed securities, warrants, and disinvestment in the public sector. The debt market of India, though large and next in size only to Japan in Asia, lacked vibrancy and did not provide adequate options for meeting medium- to long-term funds required for Greenfield projects, in particular. Infrastructure funding (essential for continued high economic growth) has become an issue in the absence of a vibrant debt market.

5.1.2. New Issue Market

The capital market, which is concerned with demand and supply of long-term funds, is dichotomized into primary or new issue market and secondary or stock exchange. The New Issue Market deals with new securities offered to the investing public while the Stock Exchange deals with the existing securities. The joint stock companies raise funds from new issue market but such new issues are also listed with stock markets which provide them regular market, ensure regular valuation and stability in prices of such securities, safety in dealings of the securities, channelize funds in the desired directions and ensure wider ownership of the securities.

As stated earlier, the new issue market plays a vital role in mobilizing funds from savers to entrepreneurs who seek to establish new enterprises or to carry out expansion/ diversification / modernization of existing ones. This may be done by issue of fresh equity or preference shares at par or premium, issue of debentures convertible and non convertible, issue of cumulative convertible preference shares or issue shares or debenture through public issue, private placement while the existing enterprises may issue shares as rights or bonus as well.

The new issues, placed first in the new issue market, can be disposed of subsequently in the stock exchange. The stock exchange provides the mechanism for regular and continuous purchase and sale of securities. This facility is of immense utility to potential investors who are assured that they may be able to dispose of the allotment of shares at any time. Thus the two markets are complementary in nature. Both the markets are connected to each other even at the time of new issue. The companies, which make new issue, apply for listing of shares on a recognized stock exchange. Listing of shares adds prestige to the firm and widens the market for the investors. The companies, which want stock exchange listing, have to comply with statutory rules and regulations of the stock exchange to ensure fair dealings in them. The stock exchanges, thus, exercise considerable control over the organization of new issues.

1) Functions of New Issue Market

As stated earlier, the main function of new issue market is to facilitate transfer of resources from savers to the users. The savers are individuals, commercial banks, insurance company etc. The users are public limited companies and the government. The new issue market plays an important role of transferring shares for production purposes, an important requisite for economic growth. It is not only a platform for raising finance to establish new enterprises but also for expansion/ diversification/ modernization of existing units. NIM performs three main functions which include

1. Origination
2. Underwriting and
3. Distribution.

a) Origination

It refers to the work of investigation, analysis and processing of new project proposals. This function starts before an issue is actually floated in the market. There are two aspects of this function. A careful study of the technical, economic and financial viability is necessary to ensure soundness of the project. This is a preliminary investigation undertaken by the sponsors of the issue. The other aspect is advisory services, which improve the quality of capital issues and ensure its success. The function of origination is done by merchant bankers who may be commercial banks, all India financial institutions or private firms.

b) Underwriting

It is an agreement whereby the underwriter promises to subscribe to a specified number of shares or debentures or a specified quantity of stock in the event of public not subscribing to the issue. If the issue is fully subscribed, then there is no liability for the underwriter. If a part of share issues remain unsold, the underwriter will buy the unsold shares.

c) Distribution

Distribution is the function of sale of securities to ultimate investors. This service is performed by brokers and agents who maintain regular and direct contact with the ultimate investors.

2) Designing the Instrument

A wide array of financial instruments designed for varying risk-reward levels and liquidity preferences have been developed. Designing of financial products calls for exacting skills in financial engineering. The limitations imposed by the legal framework have also to be taken into consideration. There are various factors that influence the choice of instrument decision and a few of which are listed below:

a) Purpose of the Offer

While designing an issue, the purpose for which the issue is made will largely determine the type of security to be used. Tangible assets are more readily financed by debt while growth opportunities which involve intangible assets such as intellectual property rights are better financed with equity.

b) Debt Servicing

The choice of security issued is also dictated by the ability of the firm to service periodic payments for the interest and principal for debt securities. While debt securities help in leveraging the firm's earnings per share, it also entails the additional financial risk of not being able to meet future obligations. The lead manager should weigh the pros and cons before deciding on the selection of the security.

c) Tax Considerations

The tax implications to the issuer and the investor should be examined. The implications vary depending on the nature of the instrument. In case of debt instruments, the amount of interest paid is tax-deductible to the issuer. However, the amount of interest received is taxable for the investor. The issuer has to pay a special dividend tax on the amount distributed as dividends also. However, the dividends are totally tax free for the investor.

d)Credit Rating

The riskiness of the firm also has an impact on the debt/equity choice. Firms whose debt issues have high ratings will be able to borrow at a lower interest cost. Such firms may also be able to price favorably their equity issues. The best alternative would be based on the precise impact of the choice of debt/equity on the firm's projected EPS and its effect on expected stock price.

e) Asset Cover

Lenders of debt normally insist on adequate security. Debt securities, secured and backed by tangible assets, are more attractive to lenders. Debenture/bond trustees often indicate the minimum asset cover. Therefore, companies without adequate asset cover are forced to issue equity.

f) Dilution of Ownership

Equity offers dilute the ownership control of the promoter group. Companies susceptible to takeover threats prefer issuing debt to equity.

3) Innovations in Financial Instruments

In the recent past, there have been innovations in the financial instruments witnessed by the Indian capital market, owing mainly to the liberalization measures. The various instruments of issues are as follows.

i) Secured Premium Notes with Detachable Warrants (SPN)

Secured Premium Notes are issued along with a detachable warrant. The warrant attached to it ensures the holder the right to apply and get equity shares after a notified period provided the Notes are fully paid up. The investor can dispose of the Secured Premium Notes on allotment at premium if the share of the issuing company commands a high premium in the market.

ii) Equity Shares with Detachable Warrants

In this instrument, along with fully paid up equity shares, detachable warrants are issued, which entifie the warrant holder to apply for a specified number of shares at a pre- determined price. Detachable warrants are registered separately with the stock exchange and traded separately.

iii) Preference Shares with Warrants

This instrument shall carry a certain number of warrants entitling the holder to apply for equity shares "at premium" at any time in one or more stages between the third and fifth year from the date of allotment.

iv) Non-Convertible Debentures with Detachable Equity Warrants

The holder of this instrument is given an option to buy a specified number of shares from the company at a predetermined price within definite time frame. There is a specific lock in period after which the holder can exercise his option to apply for equity shares.

v) Fully Convertible Cumulative Preference Shares

This instrument has two parts. The first part is convertible into equity shares automatically on the date of allotment without application by the allotee. The second part will be redeemed at par/converted into equity after a lock in period at the option of the investors.

vi) Zero Interest Fully Convertible Debentures (FCDs)

This instrument has no interest paid to the holders of this instrument fill the lock in period. After a notified period, these debentures will be automatically and compulsorily converted into shares. Before the conversion of FCDs into equity, if the company issues rights, it would be available to the holders in the proportion decided by the company. vii) Fully Convertible Debentures (FCDs) with Interest

This instrument carries no interest for a specified period. After this period, option is given to apply for equities at premium for which no additional amount is payable. However, interest on FCDs is payable at a pre-determined rate from the date of first conversion, second and last conversion and equity will be issued in lieu of interest amount.

viii) Zero Interest Partly Convertible Debentures (FCDs)

Zero Interest Partly Convertible Debentures (FCDs) with Detachable and Separately Tradable Warrants. This partly convertible debentures has two parts. The first part is convertible into equity shares at a fixed amount on the date of allotment. The second part is non-convertible and redeemed at par at the end of a specific period. The second part will also carry a detachable and separately tradable warrant.

ix) Zero Interest Bonds

The instrument is sold at a discount from their eventual maturity value and bears no interest. In India, companies issue zero interest convertible bonds. These bonds do not carry any interest till the date of conversion and are converted into equity shares at par or premium on the expiry of fixed period.

x) Deep Discount Bonds

These types of bonds are sold at a large discount to their nominal value. There is no interest payment on these bonds and the investors get returns as accretion to the par value of the instrument over its life.

xi) Option Bonds

Option bonds may be cumulative or non- cumulative as per the option of the holder of the bonds. In case of cumulative bonds, interest is accumulated and is payable on maturity only. In case of non- cumulative bonds, the interest is paid periodically.

xii) Bonds with Warrants

A warrant allows the holder to buy a number of equity shares at a pre- specified price in future. The warrants are usually attached to debentures or preference shares issued by companies as sweetener to make issues more attractive.

4) Functionaries in the New Issue Market

The functionaries in the new issue market are those concerned with the formation of joint stock companies and the issue of their securities to the public. There are many functionaries in the new issue market. The important of them are discussed below.

A) Merchant Bankers

The financial institutions in India could not meet the demand for long term funds required by the ever-expanding industry and trade. The corporate sector, therefore, meet their requirements through issue of shares and debentures in the capital market. To raise money from the capital market, promoters depend upon merchant bankers who manage the whole show by rendering multifarious services. The merchant bankers also advise the investors of the incentives available in the form of tax reliefs and statutory obligations. They help the company in carrying out functions related to new issues, such as determination of security - mix to be issued, drafting of prospectus, application forms, allotment letters and a host of other documents, appointment of registrars for handling share applications and transfers, making arrangements for underwriting, placement of shares, selection and appointment of brokers and bankers to the issue, publicity of the issue, etc.

B) Promoters

Modem industrial enterprises require large amount of capital which can be raised only by resorting to the joint stock form of organization. Company promoters and syndicates do the work of establishing a joint stock company. It is the promoter who is responsible for conception or discovery of the idea to exploit the possibility of some industrial proposition.

They work up details, formulate the financial plan which they usually do with the help of an issue house and finally they have to procure funds to put the proposition into active operation.

In case the company is successfully established and investors come forth to take up its shares, the promoter is duly rewarded. If the venture fails, he stands to lose not only his money he had sunk in the venture but his reputation as well. The promoters, in the case of projects of large dimensions, form a syndicate. All members of the syndicate work up the possibilities of the proposition and undertake the investigation and examination of the scheme. After completing the financial plan, the work of drawing up the prospectus, the memorandum of association and articles of association for the formal incorporation as a company is launched. After all the formalities are completed, the new company is ready to be launched and its issue is to be placed before the public.

C) Underwriters

Underwriting is an agreement whereby certain parties assure the issuing company to take up shares, debentures or other securities to a specified extent in case the public subscription does not come up to the expected levels. It is necessary for a public company, which invites public subscription for its securities to ensure that its issue is fully subscribed. The company cannot depend on its advertisements to bring in the full subscription. Usually the underwriters can be divided into two categories, namely, Financial Institutions and Banks, on the one hand, and Broker - Underwriters and Approved Investment Companies / Trusts, on the other.

D) Registrars

The Registrars, sometimes also called the "Issue House", are responsible normally for receiving the share applications from various collection centers through controlling branches of bankers to the issue, analyzing them, recommending the basis of allotment, in consultation with the managers to the regional stock exchanges, for approval, arranging for dispatch of allotment letters and preparing the register of members etc. Their job normally starts with the opening of the subscription list and continues till the share certificates are dispatched.

E) Brokers

Brokers are the people who actually bring the prospective investors and the company together. It may not be an exaggeration to state that success or failure of a public issue depends to a large extent on the strategy of the brokers. Generally, they are members of recognized stock exchanges. With a view to providing better and professional services to investing public and to promote development of capital market on healthy lines, the Government has since allowed multiple membership to members of stock exchanges and accorded recognition to corporate entities and financial institutions including subsidiaries of the banks.

F) Bankers

The commercial banks receive the share application money along with the share application forms from the prospective investors. Depending upon the size of the issue, at least 4 or 5 banks are designated as bankers to the issue. Different branches of these banks are named at various locations where such application money is accepted. These collecting branches send the application forms and money received by them to a specified branch called "Controlling Branch".

G) Financial Institutions

The financial institutions at the time of sanctioning underwriting support/ term loans to the company, usually stipulate that they approve the draft of the prospectus and also the proposed programme for public issue. There are three principal All India Financial Institutions - IDBl, IFCI and ICICI. Even when all the three institutions jointly finance a project under their participating finance scheme, one of them is generally chosen as the "Lead Financial Institution" which acts on behalf of the other two. Hence it is generally adequate if the company obtains the necessary approval only from the Regional Office of the Lead Institution. Therefore an advance copy of the draft prospectus is sent to them with a request to forward their comments, if any, direct to the Lead Institution.

H) Publicity and Advertising Agents

Public issue is an effort to motivate and persuade members of the public to invest in the shares of the company. It is, therefore, essential that the general public is made aware of the company, its activities, its plans for future, etc. It is of vital importance that publicity is given before the public issue by giving Newspaper and TV Advertisements. Press Releases, Press/ Brokers' Conference, Leaflets, Brochures, Posters and even Audio-Visual Shows are the usual media of publicity used for the public issue. There are some advertising agencies which specialize in financial advertising and publicity campaign for public issues.

I) Government Statutory Agencies

Besides the various agencies which are directly connected with a public issue, there are some statutory/government agencies that are connected with public issue. These are:

(1) SEBI which provides guidelines for public issue, (2) Registrar of the Companies with whom the prospectus has to be filed and registered before the public issue under Section 60 of

the Companies Act, 1956, (3) Reserve Bank of India from whom necessary permission has to be obtained for non-resident investment, if any, in the company, (4) The Stock Exchange where the company's shares/debentures are to be listed,(5) Industrial Licensing Authorities for necessary industrial license to be obtained for the project or other statutory bodies like DGTD etc, with whom the capacity of the project has to be registered, and (6) Pollution Control Authorities and other Local Authorities from whom the clearance may have to be obtained and such clearance is mentioned in the prospectus.

J) Other Agencies

In addition, the company will also have interaction with other agencies like auditors, legal advisers, taxation or technical experts whose names or statements are mentioned or quoted in the prospectus.

5) Mechanism of New Issues

The following are the mechanism of new issues

1. Public Issue Through Prospectus
2. Offer for Sale
3. Initial Public Offers (IPOs) through Secondary Market
4. Rights Issue
5. Bonus Issues
6. Tender Method
7. Over The Counter Placement(OTCEI)
8. Stock Option
9. Book Building
10. Green Shoe Option
11. Private Placement and
12. e - IPOs

a) Public Issue through Prospectus

This is the most common method of issue of securities by companies. Under this method, the company issues a prospectus which is an invitation to the investing public for subscription. It is a direct offer by the issuing company to the general public to subscribe to the securities of the company at a stated price. Public issue through prospectus is underwritten to safeguard against an unsatisfactory response from the public. The prospectus contains the following information.

1. Company's name and address of its registered office
2. Names and addresses of the company's promoters, manager, managing director, directors, company secretary, legal adviser, auditors, bankers, brokers, etc
3. Date of opening and closing of subscription list
4. Contents of articles or any contract relating to terms and conditions of appointment of managing director or manager
5. Names and addresses of underwriters, the amount underwritten and the underwriting commission
6. Material details regarding the project i.e. location, plant and machinery, technology, collaboration, performance guarantee, infrastructure facilities etc
7. Nature of products, marketing set-up, export potential and obligations
8. Past performance and future prospects
9. Management's perception regarding risk factor
10. Credit rating obtained from CRISIL or any other recognized rating agency
11. Statement that the company will make an application to specified stock exchange(s) for listing its securities, and so on.

b) Offer for Sale

Under this method, the company does not directly offer its shares to the public but through intermediaries, brokers. The issue is also underwritten to avoid the possibility of the issue largely remaining with the issue houses. Sale of securities, in this case, is done in two stages. In the first stage, the issuing company makes an en bloc sale of securities to the issue houses or stockbrokers at an agreed fixed price. The second stage involves re-sale of these securities by issue houses or stockbrokers to ultimate investors at a higher price. The issuing houses have to meet various expenses such as, underwriting commission, prospectus cost, advertisement expenses, etc,

c) Initial Public Offers (IPOs) through Secondary Market

This system is the reverse of the secondary market wherein brokers place orders on behalf of clients through a special window on the trading terminal. After the basis of allocation is finalized and brokers advised on the success of applications, successful allottees submit the application form and the amount payable through the broker to the clearinghouse. Subsequently, the share certificates would be delivered to the investors by creating the depository account in the name of the investor.

d) Rights Issue

Rights issue is an invitation to the existing shareholders to subscribe for additional shares to be issued by a company. Rights simply means an option to buy certain securities at a certain privileged price within a certain specified period. Section 81 of the Companies Act, 1956 has provided for a pre-emptive privilege to the existing shareholders of a company to purchase shares in the further issue of the company.

e) Bonus Issues

Issue of bonus shares does not result in raising ft-esh capital. It is merely a conversion of existing reserves and surpluses into share capital. It represents just a book entry subject to certain rules and regulations. Total resource base of the company does not change due to issue of bonus shares. Choice of issue mechanism is influenced by the resources at the command of the issuer, the size of the issue, the type of securities issued, and market standing of the group and/ or the company making the issue and the market sentiments at the time of issue.

f) Tender Method

Under the tender method of marketing the securities, the issue price is not predetermined. The company announces the public issue without indicating the issue price and invites bids from various interested parties. The parties participating in the tender submit their maximum offers indicating the maximum price they are willing to pay as well as the number of shares they are willing to buy.

g) Over the Counter Placement (OTCEI)

The Over the Counter Exchange of India began its operations as second tier bourse only in 1992. It permits smaller companies to raise funds. The procedure involved under this method is that the company wishing to raise capital through OTC Exchange appoints a member of the OTCEI as sponsor. The sponsor appraises the project and values the shares of the company. The sponsor ensures the success of the issue even if it has to subscribe to all the shares by itself The OTCEI members and dealers operate counters to facilitate trading with the investing public.

h) Stock Option

Employees Stock Option Scheme (ESOP) is a voluntary scheme on the part of the company to encourage employees to participate in the company. The scheme also offers an incentive to the employees to stay in the company. The scheme is particularly useful in case of companies whose business activity is dominantly based on the talent of the employees.

i) Book Building

The aim of Book Building is to price the issue as high as possible but it cannot be so high that the investor loses interest. On the lower side, the issue price should not be lower than what the investor is willing to shell out.

j) Green Shoe Option (GSO)

SEBI has recently introduced Green Shoe Option (GSO), a new phenomenon for Indian investors. A company making an Initial Public Offer (IPO) through the Book Building mechanism can hold the GSO. This is an option that allows underwriter of an Initial Public Offering to sell additional shares to the public. The objective of introducing GSO by SEBI is to create a safety net for investors who participate in the initial public offer of a company. It is to be used as a mechanism to stabilize the post-listing share price. The introduction of GSO came at a time when primary market in India was going through a bad phase. The IPOs were overpriced and prices used to fall after listing on the stock exchanges. This hurt the retail investors as it created a loss immediately on listing. As a result, investors were shying away from the primary market.

k) Private Placement

The private placement involves issue of securities, debt or equity, to a limited number of subscribers, such as banks, FIs, MPs and high net worth individuals. It is arranged through a merchant/ investment banker, who acts as an agent of the issuer and brings together the issuer and the investor(s) on the presumption that these are allotted to a few sophisticated and experienced investors and the public at large are not taken into confidence. The securities offered in a private placement are exempt from the public disclosure regulations and registration requirements of the regulatory body. What distinguishes private placement from public issue is that while the latter invite application from many subscribers, the subscription in the private placement are normally restricted to a limited number.

l) e-IPOs

A company proposing to issue capital to public through online system of the stock exchange has to comply with section 55 to 68A of the Companies Act, 1956 and SEBI (DIP) Guidelines 2000. The company is required to enter into an agreement with the stock exchange(s), which have the requisite system for on-line offer of securities. The agreement should cover rights, duties, responsibilities and obligations of the company and the stock exchanges inter-se, with provision for a dispute resolution mechanism between the company and the stock exchange.

The issuer company appoints a registrar to the issue having electronic connectivity with the stock exchanges. The issuer company can apply for listing of its securities at any exchange through which it offers its securities to public through on- line system, apart from the requirement of listing on the regional stock exchange. The stock exchange appoints brokers for the purpose of accepting applications and placing orders with the company. The lead manager would co- ordinate all the activities amongst various intermediaries connected to the system.

From the above discussion it is understood that new issue market plays an important role in mobilizing fund from savers. It is a platform to raise finance for expansion, diversification and modernization of existing unit. Introduction of new innovative financial instruments in the new issue market minimizes the risk and maximizes the returns. In recent past there has been a lot of innovations taking place in the financial instruments with the objective of liberalizing the existing measures. On the other hand, functionaries in the new issue market have also gradually increased and it increases the competitiveness among the market players (functionaries).

5.2. Sources of Long Term Finance

The main sources of long term finance are as follows:

1. Shares

These are issued to the general public. These may be of two types:

(i) Equity and (ii) Preference. The holders of shares are the owners of the business.

2. Debentures

These are also issued to the general public. The holders of debentures are the creditors of the company.

3. Public Deposits

General public also like to deposit their savings with a popular and well established company which can pay interest periodically and pay-back the deposit when due.

4. Retained Earnings

The company may not distribute the whole of its profits among its shareholders. It may retain a part of the profits and utilize it as capital.

5. Term Loans from Banks

Many industrial development banks, cooperative banks and commercial banks grant medium term loans for a period of three to five years.

6. Loan from Financial Institutions

There are many specialized financial institutions established by the Central and State governments which give long term loans at reasonable rate of interest. Some of these institutions are: Industrial Finance Corporation of India (IFCI), Industrial Development Bank of India (IDBI), Industrial Credit and Investment Corporation of India (ICICI), Unit Trust of India (UTI), and State Finance Corporations etc.

5.2.1. Shares

Issue of shares is the main source of long term finance. Shares are issued by joint stock companies to the public. A company divides its capital into units of a definite face value, say of Rs. 10 each or Rs. 100 each. Each unit is called a share. A person holding shares is called a shareholder.

Characteristics of Shares

The main characteristics of shares are following:

1. It is a unit of capital of the company
2. Each share is of a definite face value.
3. A share certificate is issued to a shareholder indicating the number of shares and the amount.
4. Each share has a distinct number.
5. The face value of a share indicates the interest of a person in the company and the extent of his liability.
6. Shares are transferable units.

Investors are of different habits and temperaments. Some want to take lesser risk and are interested in a regular income. There are others who may take greater risk in anticipation of huge profits in future. In order to tap the savings of different types of people, a company may issue different types of shares. These are:

1. Preference shares, and
2. Equity Shares.

Preference Shares

Preference Shares are the shares which carry preferential rights over the equity shares. These rights are (a) receiving dividends at a fixed rate, (b) getting back the capital in case the company is wound-up. Investment in these shares are safe, and a preference shareholder also gets dividend regularly.

Equity Shares

Equity shares are shares which do not enjoy any preferential right in the matter of payment of dividend or repayment of capital. The equity shareholder gets dividend only after the payment of dividends to the preference shares. There is no fixed rate of dividend for equity shareholders. The rate of dividend depends upon the surplus profits. In case of winding up of a company, the equity share capital is refunded only after refunding the preference share capital. Equity shareholders have the right to take part in the management of the company. However, equity shares also carry more risk. Following are the merits and demerits of equity shares:

(a) Merits

(A) To the Shareholders

1. In case there are good profits, the company pays dividend to the equity shareholders at a higher rate.
2. The value of equity shares goes up in the stock market with the increase in profits of the concern.
3. Equity shares can be easily sold in the stock market.
4. Equity shareholders have greater say in the management of a company as they are conferred voting rights by the Articles of Association.

(B) To the Management

1. A company can raise fixed capital by issuing equity shares without creating any charge on its fixed assets.
2. The capital raised by issuing equity shares is not required to be paid back during the life time of the company. It will be paid back only if the company is wound up.
3. There is no liability on the company regarding payment of dividend on equity shares. The company may declare dividends only if there are enough profits.
4. If a company raises more capital by issuing equity shares, it leads to greater confidence among the investors and creditors.

Demerits

(A) To the Shareholders

1. Uncertainly about Payment of Dividend

Equity share-holders get dividend only when the company is earning sufficient profits and the Board of Directors declare dividend. If there are preference shareholders, equity shareholders get dividend only after payment of dividend to the preference shareholders.

2. Speculative

Often there is speculation on the prices of equity shares. This is particularly so in times of boom when dividend paid by the companies is high.

3. Danger of Over-capitalization

In case the management miscalculates the long term financial requirements, it may raise more funds than required by issuing shares. This may amount to over-capitalization which in turn leads to low value of shares in the stock market.

4. Ownership in Name Only

Holding of equity shares in a company makes the holder one of the owners of the company. Such shareholders enjoy voting rights. They manage and control the company. But then it is all in theory. In practice, a handful of persons control the votes and manage the company. Moreover, the decision to declare dividend rests with the Board of Directors.

5. Higher Risk

Equity shareholders bear a very high degree of risk. In case of losses they do not get dividend. In case of winding up of a company, they are the very last to get refund of the money invested. Equity shares actually swim and sink with the company.

B) To the Management

1. No Trading on Equity

Trading on equity means ability of a company to raise funds through preference shares, debentures and bank loans etc. On such funds the company has to pay at a fixed rate. This enables equity shareholders to enjoy a higher rate of return when profits are large. The major part of the profit earned is paid to the equity shareholders because borrowed funds carry only a fixed rate of interest. But if a company has only equity shares and does not have either preference shares, debentures or loans, it cannot have the advantage of trading on equity.

2. Conflict of Interests

As the equity shareholders carry voting rights, groups are formed to corner the votes and grab the control of the company. There develops conflict of interests which is harmful for the smooth functioning of a company.

Difference between preference shares and equity shares

We have learnt the meaning and the feature of preference and equity shares. Now we can differentiate between the two.

Basis of Preference Shares Equity shares difference

1. Choice It is not compulsory to It is compulsory to issue these shares. issue these shares.
2. Payment Dividend is paid on Dividend is paid on of dividend: these shares in these shares only preference to the after paying dividend equity shares. on preference shares.
3. Return In case of winding Capital on these shares of capital up of a company is refunded in case the capital is of winding up of refunded in the company after preference over refund of preference the equity shares. share capital.

5.2.2. Debentures

Whenever a company wants to borrow a large amount of fund for a long but fixed period, it can borrow from the general public by issuing loan certificates called Debentures. The total amount to be borrowed is divided into units of fixed amount say of Rs.100 each. These units are called Debentures. These are offered to the public to subscribe in the same manner as is done in the case of shares. A debenture is issued under the common seal of the company. It is a written acknowledgement of money borrowed. It specifies the terms and conditions, such as rate of interest, time repayment, security offered, etc.

Characteristics of Debenture

Following are the characteristics of Debentures:

1. Debenture holders are the creditors of the company. They are entitled to periodic payment of interest at a fixed rate.
2. Debentures are repayable after a fixed period of time, say five years or seven years as per agreed terms.
3. Debenture holders do not carry voting rights.
4. Ordinarily, debentures are secured. In case the company fails to pay interest on debentures or repay the principal amount, the debenture holders can recover it from the sale of the assets of the company.

Types of Debentures

Debentures may be classified as:

a) Redeemable Debentures and Irredeemable Debentures

b) Convertible Debentures and Non-convertible Debentures.

Redeemable Debentures

These are debentures repayable on a pre-determined date or at any time prior to their maturity, provided the company so desires and gives a notice to that effect.

Irredeemable Debentures

These are also called perpetual debentures. A company is not bound to repay the amount during its life time. If the issuing company fails to pay the interest, it has to redeem such debentures.

Convertible Debentures

The holders of these debentures are given the option to convert their debentures into equity shares at a time and in a ratio as decided by the company.

Non-convertible Debentures

These debentures cannot be converted into shares.

Merits of Debentures

Following are some of the advantages of debentures:

1. *Raising Funds Without Allowing Control over the Company*

Debenture holders have no right either to vote or take part in the management of the company.

2. *Reliable Source of Long Term Finance*

Since debentures are ordinarily issued for a fixed period, the company can make the best use of the money. It helps long term planning.

3. *Tax Benefits*

Interest paid on debentures is treated as an expense and is charged to the profits of the company. The company thus saves income tax.

4. *Investors' Safety*

Debentures are mostly secured. On winding up of the company, they are repayable before any payment is made to the shareholders. Interest on debentures is payable irrespective of profit or loss.

Demerits

Following are the Demerits of Debentures

1. As the interest on debentures has to be paid every year whether there are profits or not, it becomes burdensome in case the company incurs losses.
2. Usually the debentures are secured. The company creates a charge on its assets in favour of debenture holders. So a company which does not own enough fixed assets cannot borrow money by issuing debentures. Moreover, the assets of the company once mortgaged cannot be used for further borrowing.
3. Debenture-finance enables a company to trade on equity. But too much of such finance leaves little for shareholders, as most of the profits may be required to pay interest on debentures. This brings frustration in the minds of shareholders and the value of shares may fall in the securities markets.
4. Burdensome in times of depression: During depression the profits of the company decline. It may be difficult to pay interest on debentures. As interest goes on accumulating, it may lead to the closure of the company. Until now you have learnt about issue of shares and debentures as two main sources of raising long term finance. You have also learnt about the merits and demerits of the two. Now let us make a comparative study of shares and debentures for raising long term capital.

Basis Shares Debentures

1. Status Shareholders are the Debenture holders owners of the company. are the creditors of
2. They provide ownership the company. They capital which is not provide loans refundable generally for a fixed period. Such loans are to be paid back.
3. Nature of Shareholders get Interest is paid return on dividends. The amount on debentures investment is not fixed. It depends at a fixed rate. on the profit of the Interest is company. Hence only payable even those persons invest in if the company is shares who are ready to running at a loss. So take risk. it is good investment for those who do not want to
4. Rights Share holders are the Debenture holders do real owners of the not have the right company. They have to attend meetings the right to vote and of the company. So frame the objectives they have no say in and policies of the the management of company. the company.
5. Therefore sufficient fixed assets are required when debentures are to be issued.

6. Order of Shareholders take the Debenture holders repayment. Maximum risk because have the priority of their capital will be repayment over paid back only after shareholders. Repaying the loan of debenture holders.

5.2.3. Term Loans

A term loan is a monetary loan that is repaid in regular payments over a set period of time. Term loans usually last between one and ten years, but may last as long as 30 years in some cases. A term loan usually involves an unfixed interest rate that will add additional balance to be repaid.

Term loans can be given on an individual basis, but are often used for small business loans. The ability to repay over a long period of time is attractive for new or expanding enterprises, as the assumption is that they will increase their profit over time. Term loans are a good way of quickly increasing capital in order to raise a business' supply capabilities or range. For instance, some new companies may use a term loan to buy company vehicles or rent more space for their operations.

Considerations

One thing to consider when getting a term loan is whether the interest rate is fixed or floating. A fixed interest rate means that the percentage of interest will never increase, regardless of the financial market. Low-interest periods are usually an excellent time to take out a fixed rate loan. Floating interest rates will fluctuate with the market, which can be good or bad for you depending on what happens with the global and national economy. Since some term loans last for 10 years, betting that the rate will stay consistently low is a real risk.

Also, consider whether the term loan you are looking at uses compound interest. If it does, the amount of interest will be periodically added to the principal borrowed amount, meaning that the interest keeps getting higher the longer the term lasts. If the loan does use compound interest, check to see if there are any penalties for early repayment of the loan. If you get a windfall or profits increase spectacularly, you may be able to pay off your entire balance before it is due, preventing you from paying additional interest by waiting for the loan term to end.

5.2.4. Lease

A lease is a contractual arrangement calling for the lessee (user) to pay the lessor (owner) for use of an asset. Property, buildings and vehicles are common assets that are leased. Industrial or business equipment is also leased.

Broadly put, a lease agreement is a contract between two parties, the lessor and the lessee. The lessor is the legal owner of the asset; the lessee obtains the right to use the asset in return for regular rental payments. The lessee also agrees to abide by various conditions regarding their use of the property or equipment. For example, a person leasing a car may agree that the car will only be used for personal use.

The narrower term rental agreement can be used to describe a lease in which the asset is tangible property. Language used is that the user rents the land or goods let out or rented out by the owner. The verb to lease is less precise because it can refer to either of these actions. Examples of a lease for intangible property are use of a computer program (similar to a license, but with different provisions), or use of a radio frequency (such as a contract with a cell-phone provider).

5.2.5. Hire Purchase

A hire purchase is a method of buying goods through making installment payments over time. The term "hire purchase" originated in the United Kingdom and is similar to rent-to-own arrangements in the United States. Under a hire purchase contract, the buyer is leasing the goods and does not obtain ownership until the full amount of the contract is paid.

'Hire Purchase'

To begin a hire purchase, a payment is often required up front. The rest of the amount due is submitted through scheduled payments, similar to an installment loan or a vehicle lease. The ownership of the good purchased through a hire purchase is not officially transferred to the buyer until all required payments have been submitted. Companies offering hire purchase options earn a profit by applying additional costs to the monthly payment which serves as interest charges for the purchase.

5.2.6. Venture Capital Financing

Venture capital financing is a type of financing by venture capital. It is private equity capital provided as seed funding to early-stage, high-potential, growth companies (startup companies) or more often it is after the seed funding round as a growth funding round (also referred to as series A round). It is provided in the interest of generating a return on investment through an eventual realization event such as an IPO or trade sale of the company.

5.2.7. Private Equity

Private equity is capital that is not noted on a public exchange. Private equity is composed of funds and investors that directly invest in private companies, or that engage in buyouts of public companies, resulting in the delisting of public equity. Institutional and retail investors provide the capital for private equity, and the capital can be utilized to fund new technology, make acquisitions, expand working capital, and to bolster and solidify a balance sheet.

'Private Equity'

Private equity comes primarily from institutional investors and accredited investors, who can dedicate substantial sums of money for extended time periods. In most cases, considerably long holding periods are often required for private equity investments, in order to ensure a turnaround for distressed companies or to enable liquidity events such as an initial public offering (IPO) or a sale to a public company.

Since the 1970s, the private equity market has strengthened readily. Pools of funds are sometimes created by private equity firms in order to privatize extra-large companies. A significant number of private equity firms perform actions known as leveraged buyouts (LBOs). Through LBOs, substantial amounts of money are provided in order to finance large purchases. After this transaction, private equity firms attempt to improve the prospects, profits and overall financial health of the company, with the ultimate goal being a resale of the company to a different firm or cashing out through an IPO.

Fees and Profits

The fee structure for private equity firms typically varies, but usually includes a management fee and a performance fee. Certain firms charge a 2% management fee annually on managed assets and require 20% of the profits gained from the sale of a company.

www.ingramcontent.com/pod-product-compliance
Lightning Source LLC
Chambersburg PA
CBHW071345230926
51846CB00002B/457
* 9 7 8 9 3 8 7 8 6 2 2 8 9 *